IDENTITY HEIST

CHILLING ACCOUNTS OF TORTURE, KIDNAPPING,
AND LEGAL LOOPHOLES UNLEASHING CHAOS
ACROSS THE US & THE WORLD

LINDSAY MCGUIRE

DISCLAIMER

Read at your own risk. Engage with care. This book contains depictions of war crimes, domestic violence, coercive control, legal abuse, psychological trauma, and systemic failures. It is not intended for all audiences. Reader discretion is strongly advised.

The narrative is based on real events and survivor testimony. Names, timelines, and locations have been modified to preserve anonymity and narrative flow. While every effort has been made to present accurate reflections of systemic patterns and lived experiences, this is a work of creative nonfiction rooted in advocacy, not clinical or legal advice.

Caveat lector.

The publisher and author assume no liability for the reader's interpretation, emotional response, or actions taken in response to this content. Engagement with this material is voluntary. You, the reader, accept full responsibility for your participation in these pages.

This is not a safe book.

But neither is the world it exposes.

Dedication

For the Countless Others who did Not make it Out alive

And

To the Others

Still

Struggling to Breathe.

Quotes and Hope's Blessing

"Every truth is a kindness, even if it makes others uncomfortable. Every untruth is an unkindness, even if it makes others comfortable." – Glennon Doyle, *Untamed.*

"In the 1953 episode of the television series *Dragnet*, created and portrayed by Jack Webb, Sgt. Joe Friday tells the main suspect, "All we know are the facts." *This* line is often misremembered *as* "Just the facts." The same meaning applies to this account; facts blurred with fiction to shield the innocent are all laid before you.

As you read these pages, this humble journal asks you, dear reader, to let these truths reach your heart, which is still alive and capable of feeling. My own emotions have been numbed and blurred by the normalized and legalized theft and erasure of identities. Yet, I hope that yours can rise to the surface.

With this blessing and my deepest gratitude, I respectfully ask for your attention and action.

~ Hope Livingston

Table of Contents

Preface

By Jonathon Kendall

This book wasn't written to make you comfortable.

It was written because someone needed to tell the truth—about how abuse hides behind court orders, religious language, and official seals.

About how easy it is to look the other way.

And maybe, if you're like me, you didn't realize how deep it goes. Maybe you thought you understood.

I didn't... not until this. Now, I can't unsee it.

Identity Heist is not a typical story. It doesn't provide neat answers or easy endings.

Instead, it tells the truth:

About how abusers manipulate the system to maintain power.

About how women and children fall through cracks that were never meant to hold them.

About how emotional violence can be more invisible—and more lasting—than bruises.

The story reads like fiction, but it's all true.

The manipulation, the legal loopholes, the heartbreak, the terror... It's real.

In these pages, you'll witness the emotional, legal, and psychological warfare that survivors of abuse face—not just from their abusers, but from the very institutions meant to protect them.

This book doesn't follow a clean arc of justice. It's messy. It's painful. And it's necessary.

It's for those who've lived it. And for those who've never seen it—until now.

As a man, I've been in rooms where these conversations never happen. I've benefited from systems I didn't fully understand.

But this story changed me. It made me confront truths I could no longer ignore.

Because I realized how many times I'd asked the wrong questions: "Why didn't she leave?" "Why didn't she call the police?" "Why didn't someone help?" This book answered all of those questions.

And it changed how I listen.

The author guides us into a world most people never see unless they're living it, and we owe her our attention.

To the author: thank you for your bravery, your honesty, and your trust. To the survivors reading this: I see you. I hear you. This book is for you.

To those who don't understand yet: don't turn away. Lean in. Let it change you, too.

This isn't a book to be read quickly. It's one to sit with.

If you've ever felt helpless in the face of someone else's pain, this book is for you.

If you've ever been on the outside of a story, wondering how it could happen, this book is for you.

If you've survived something no one believed, this book is for you. I hope you'll keep turning the pages.

I hope you'll ask the hard questions.

And I hope you'll come away, as I did, changed.

— Jonathon Kendall

CEO, Author, and Publisher April 2025

Introduction

More chilling than fiction, this harrowing true-life account follows the story of one family.

Identity Heist is a gripping true-crime exposé that unveils a world of domestic abuse, coercive control, and faith-based power plays lurking behind closed doors. In this unflinching narrative memoir-thriller, a survivor's real-life account blends psychological suspense with high-stakes legal drama as she navigates torture, kidnapping, and systemic injustice. From clandestine religious manipulation to hidden court loopholes, every harrowing revelation demands urgent justice reform and heightened awareness of social injustice. This heart-pounding narrative shines a light on the dark underbelly of family courts, taxpayer-funded government institutions, and political entities masquerading as religious organizations. Identity Heist and its companion book, Divine Theft, are essential reading for true-crime enthusiasts, legal advocates, and social-justice champions. Brace yourself for explosive revelations and an empowering call to action that will ignite conversations and mobilize change as Lindsay McGuire redefines the boundaries of real-life thriller storytelling.

Not just a book to be read, but to be experienced. Shall we begin?

Chapter 1

The Present Pickle: Present Day

The morning light filtered softly through the curtains, casting a gentle glow across the farmhouse that overlooked a large backyard filled with laughing children and rolling pastures. An Emily Joy song played in the distant living room, its lyrics celebrating a bright new day, but in the laundry room, time stood still. The air was cold and heavy with unspoken dread. There, amidst piles of freshly laundered clothes, lay Hope, her body unmoving—a lifeless presence in the mundane room.

Ten-year-old Anna stumbled into the laundry room, the youngest child from Hope's second marriage—the one tied to the Latter-Day Saint or Mormon organization. The words of that church felt distant now, irrelevant to what lay before her. Her breath caught in her throat as she saw her mother lying motionless on the cold floor.

For a moment, disbelief held Anna frozen, staring at the surreal sight—a scene not of dreams, but of stark, raw reality. It was a moment that would forever be etched in her memory.

"Wake up, Mom! Please!" Anna's urgent voice, tinged with desperation and sheer terror, sliced through the silence, yet the room offered no reply. Kneeling beside her mother, she shook Hope's shoulders, her small hands trembling. The house seemed to hold its breath with her, wrapped in an oppressive stillness that refused to break.

An overwhelming sense of helplessness engulfed her, an emotion too heavy for her young heart to bear alone. Tears welled up, blurring her vision as she tried to comprehend the gravity of the moment. "Mom, please..." she whispered again, hoping against hope for a response, a miracle—anything to shatter the nightmare that had become her reality.

Her breath came in ragged sobs. The smell of detergent clung to the air, sharp and sterile. Somewhere, a floorboard creaked under a sibling's footstep, but Anna couldn't turn her head. Not yet.

Her mind slipped back to a time not far in the past, perhaps as a way to detach from what she could not do now, grasping for hope of what might be. She could almost see it: the evening sun dipping below the horizon, splashes of golden light warming the cozy dining room where Hope and her seven children gathered for dinner. Laughter bubbled around the table, mingling with the clatter of dishes and silverware. It had been a rare, contented moment, filled with the simple joy of shared stories and the warmth of togetherness.

Suddenly, Anna remembered that the cheerful chatter was broken by a sharp, gasping cough. Hope's face had turned an alarming shade of red, her eyes wide with panic as her hands flew to her diaphragm. The moment had frozen around Anna—her siblings' wide-eyed fear flickering in the corner of her vision, though all she could focus on was her mother.

In that instant, time seemed to slow. Adrenaline surged through Anna's small body. Ignoring her own pounding heart and trembling hands, she rushed to Hope's side, recalling the life-saving technique she had learned by watching others save her mother before. She positioned herself behind Hope, wrapping her arms around her mother's waist in a firm grip.

"Stay calm, Mom," she whispered, more to herself than anyone else, trying to summon courage beyond her years.

With determination, she thrust her fists upward into her mother's abdomen. Once. Twice. And then—blessed relief—as a small piece of rice dislodged from her mother's throat, softly landing on the plate before them both.

The room exhaled collectively. Hope gasped for air, her color slowly returning to normal as she hugged Anna tightly. Laughter returned, this time mixed with tears of relief and awe at another miracle.

In that simple dining room, amidst the remnants of dinner, the fragility and strength of their family dynamic shone brightly. Another child in the merry household had transformed into a hero, saving their mother's life once more. In that moment, they were reminded of how intertwined their fates were— bound together by love, survival, and a shared determination to face whatever life might throw their way.

The warmth of that memory evaporated in an instant, pulled away by the cold tiles beneath Anna's knees and the chilling silence that surrounded her once more. The laundry room was back, and Hope hadn't moved. In a series of brief, punctuated thoughts, Anna's mind flitted from the present shock to hazy fragments of happier times. These fleeting memories contrasted sharply with the present horror—a reminder that even in moments of deep despair, the bonds of family persist.

Anna's piercing cries over her mother's cold body shattered the afternoon tranquility, rippling into the bright outdoors where sun-kissed leaves danced in the crisp breeze. Through the haze of her tears, Anna barely registered the shadows rushing toward her—the blurred, frightened faces of her siblings drawn by her wail, their footfalls thunderous against the wooden floors.

***

In another part of the house, Sebastian's world cracked open the moment he heard his sister's scream. The thirteen-year-old brother was the first to reach Anna and their mother's lifeless body, skidding to a halt just inside the laundry room door. Panic surged through Sebastian as he stopped short. His eyes locked on the still form of his mother, Anna's trembling body hunched beside her. His lungs forgot to breathe. Instinctively, he crouched beside her, his own heart hammering in his chest like a caged bird.

As he enveloped his sister in a tender embrace, bitter memories surged forth, unbidden. Echoes of their father Jim's rage filled his mind, words cutting through the fog of recalled terror.

"Use your head!" "Think!"

"Don't be such a baby, boy!" "Shut up—don't cry!"

"I didn't do that!"

Torrential words came back in sharp bursts, each memory stabbing through Sebastian's mind like shards of glass.

The booming voice and truth-twisting shouts of his father's knife-like words echoed in the recesses of Sebastian's thoughts. Each syllable served as a cold reminder of the volatile tempest that had too often stormed through their house, mixing in this thirteen-year-old's mind like cement. His father Jim's rageful physical and psychologically twisting outbursts were a Jekyll and Hyde experience for Sebastian and his siblings, just before finding refuge in this farmhouse with their family's last protector, provider, and rock: their mom.

Each memory was vivid—Jim's flushed face twisted in fury, his hands gesticulating wild accusations as threats lingered in the air, heavy and suffocating, with stark reminders of the furious blows that might follow, either to Sebastian himself, his siblings, or their mother. With each memory, Sebastian involuntarily relived scene after scene of Jim pinning his mother against various walls of the old house, his larger frame dominating her slight figure. At times, he could hear her collapse; each scene felt as if it were happening in the present, showcasing some of the other ways Jim asserted his dominance over the family. Chills ran down the boy's spine as he recalled those torturous echoes of witnessing his mother's futile attempts to leave— palpable reminders of the fractures that had long split their family and their lives like a poorly glued mosaic.

Yet amid the torment of his memories, young Sebastian found a glimmer of resolve in the present, and a vow silently formed deep within him. He squeezed his younger sister's shoulders, whispering promises of protection and courage. At that moment, with the weight of silence pressing down and the shadows of the past looming large, all seven siblings had found their way back into the small laundry room and huddled together—a fragile bulwark against a world that had been anything but kind.

The room felt suffocating, heavy with the unspoken dread that wrapped itself around them. Sebastian clung tighter to Anna, sensing the others crowding around. In his blurred vision, he saw Emma, her fiery spirit dimmed but still holding firm for them all. He watched Anna bury her face in their older brother Leo's shoulder. Anna's lips moved, but no sound came. Sebastian could guess what she was thinking—this wasn't just their mother's death; it was the death of their whole world.

Sebastian's eyes scanned the room, landing on Molly, clutching her twin brother Matthew. Both of them were frozen, their faces drained of color.

His chest tightened. He didn't need to ask what they were thinking—he knew.

They remembered too, just like he did. The terror of what awaited them if they were dragged back to Jim.

Then his gaze fell to Sammy, just five, the youngest. The boy sat quietly beside their mother, his tiny fingers wrapped around hers as if they could somehow bring her back. He whispered something only she could hear.

Sebastian's throat tightened.

Sammy was doing it again—just like last year when Mom hit her head on that huge clay pot. Back then, he had whispered those same soft words, believing his presence could make everything okay. Now, he whispered again, almost like a spell: "Mommy, it's okay. It's Sammy, and we're all here. It's okay. Corbin, Jemma, Fowley, and Jim are all far away. It's okay, Mommy. We're all okay."

But Mom didn't move.

Sebastian swallowed hard as something cracked inside him. Seeing Sammy like that—still believing she might wake up—was almost more than he could bear.

Emma scooped Sammy up and hugged him tightly. "You did a great job, Sammy. Mommy is so proud of you," she whispered, her voice trembling. Sebastian watched, his throat burning. Emma's strength was their anchor now, just like Mom had been. "Sammy, Mommy can't wake up anymore," Emma said gently. "Anna, you did everything just right, okay? You were brave, just like Mommy taught us." Sebastian saw Anna nod, her small shoulders shaking, and he wished he could do more—anything—to fix this.

The twins, their eyes wide with a sudden partial understanding, cried out in unison, "Mommy! She's in Heaven!"

To the outside world, this might have seemed like just another tragic case. But for the children, the story was far more complicated. Each child had escaped the suffocating grip of Mormonism—officially known as the Church of Jesus Christ of Latter-Day Saints, which was rebranded in 2023 to simply "The Latter-Day Saints," but formerly the Mormon Organization. This emblematic change masked its deeper entanglement as one of the largest financial and political institutions in America and one of the fastest-growing non-taxed organizations internationally. Beneath the comforting language of faith, it remains inextricably tied to doctrines and purposes that bear little resemblance to the Biblical Christ they have now come to know. This complex organization commandeered the very nature of God, Christianity, and Biblical truths, stripping them of all intended meaning while retaining only Sacred names—the kidnapped Bride. For those like Hope and her children who leave the Latter-Day Saint Organization and come to understand the faith-based relationship with Christianity, or even any religion, the journey is bloody, raw, and rare. Approximately 70% of those who manage to escape Latter-Day Sainthood are so spiritually wounded that they become atheists. The indoctrination of fear triumphs over faith, promoting earned salvation through strict adherence to man-made, ever- changing regimes and rules manufactured by the Latter Day Saint/Mormon Organization. This tragic approach is void of the love song that the correctly translated Bible fully reveals. LDS members like Hope and her children are taught by their Priesthood Leaders that "Questions lead to Eternal Consequences" and that all other self-proclaimed "Christians" "miss the mark" and "lack the fullness of 'Heavenly Father's' Divine revelation," along with other isolating untruths. These fear tactics leave those who do leave deeply hurt, confused, and angry at a God who, according to Scripture, created humanity "fearfully and wonderfully" and granted them "free will" within their nature. To Hope, the Lord spared her this fate. Something within her stirred, recalling the answered prayers of her past, to a non- Mormonized God, free from

Temple restrictions, who met her in life's lowest moments. She asked and listened for her next right step.

Hope had been the architect of their flight. Patiently and painstakingly, she had steered her children toward a newly unfolding refuge—a reality where the oppressive shadows of their past were beginning to part under the warming beams of grace, joy, faith, and true love's light. Together, they had started to dive into relationships with a far greater, more intimate, all-encompassing Biblical Messiah—the Savior Christ—and His boundless Father—not built on fear, but anchored in radical love.

Still, the wounds of indoctrination ran deep within each of her children, scars left by years of teachings rooted in eternal fear. Healing had only just begun.

Now, with Hope— their mother, guardian, and last earthly guide—gone, the precarious balance of their fragile new lives teetered on the edge of collapse.

Would Jim's cold ambition drag them back into the suffocating grasp they had barely escaped? The courts would allow them to be raised by an abusive parent like Jim. Each child knew this too well from their experiences with half-siblings Jemma and Fowley. Were their lives next?

The question loomed, more fearsome than any storm: Would everything Hope had fought for die with her?

Hope's resolve had been their shield. In private, she had fought unseen battles—becoming a warrior cloaked in maternal gentleness. She taught herself the language of the courts, drafted pleadings at midnight, faced judges alone, and fought for legal protection armed with nothing but prayer, grit, and the fierce love only a mother could wield. Every court victory was another thread sewn into the fragile tapestry of their safety.

Yet one critical piece remained unfinished:

The Social Security Administration, despite assurances under the H.A.L.E. Act for crime victims, had still not issued new identifiers. For three agonizing years, Hope had waited, fought, and pleaded—knowing that without those numbers, the past could find them again. And now, with Hope gone, the question grew even sharper in the hearts of the older children:

What came next?

Would the courts return them to the man whose hands and words had nearly destroyed them?

Would foster care swallow them into a system that did not know their names, their history, or their dreams?

Or—miracle of miracles—would someone from the new church family Hope had trusted rise up to shelter them, to hold onto the precious beginnings she had sacrificed everything to give?

In silent prayers and desperate wishes too fragile to voice, each child cried out the same plea:

"Please, God—don't let it all be lost. Not after everything we've gone through together. Not now. What will happen now that she's gone?"

Author's Note

Each child in this story has endured multiple layers of trauma, abuse, and neglect at the hands of those meant to protect them. You, alongside Anna, Sebastian, and their siblings of varying ages, are experiencing what they cannot yet name. Flashbacks. These are not just intrusive memories; they are echoes of scars and the primal stirrings of survival following deep injuries. Breathe and ground yourself, as Hope taught her children. Do not let yourself get lost. Every moment matters as you turn each page.

Chapter 2

The Awakening: 10 Months Past

The fluorescent lights in the hospital room cast sharp, ghostly shadows on the pale walls. The scent of antiseptic hung in the air, mingling with the steady hum of machines monitoring her fragile form. This wasn't merely a place of recovery; it was a canvas upon which Hope's true horrors would soon be painted in vivid strokes.

Every breath Hope took felt heavy with the memories she had fought to suppress but could no longer avoid.

She lay still, her body battered and broken, yet her mind refused to rest. This was not an awakening born of peace but of sudden, wrenching necessity—a reckoning.

Years ago, Hope's first husband, Corbin, had been charming, his military whites dazzling as he smiled, embodying discipline and honor. But behind that veneer lurked something monstrous. The charm faded quickly after their vows, replaced by calculated bursts of physical rage and strategic psychological warfare.

His hands, which once promised comfort, transformed into weapons trained with precision—inflicting pain not on battlefields overseas, but within the confines of their various houses, never homes, on domestic soil.

She sought salvation in the Mormon Church, now rebranded as "The Church of Jesus Christ of Latter-Day Saints," as Corbin had introduced her to its teachings, promising that its doctrine would temper his anger. Instead, the One True Church on Earth became chains, binding her to a life of submission and silence. The church leaders turned a blind eye to their full knowledge of Corbin's abuse and innumerable acts of violence against his eternal companion and wife; Corbin was careful not to leave marks. His training as a boxer in college, before his military career supporting a Counterterrorism Special Ops Unit, had taught him how to inflict crippling pain and potentially lethal injuries upon Hope without a trace.

The military, the authorities, and the church leaders all ignored Corbin's actions against Hope and their young children, Jemma and Fowley, even after their infant son was born. Hope's Priesthood leaders, with their detached and condescending advice, reminded her that her children's and her everlasting souls were at stake: *Mind your Priesthood leaders, Hope; that includes Corbin. He is your only guide to salvation, and we are supporting his Priesthood duties to your family. You remain in our prayers. Keep praying to your Heavenly Father for the Holy Ghost to guide you.*

Hope's thoughts turned to Fowley and Jemma, the children she had with Corbin. Once the light of her life, they now embodied his venom. Their threats felt like promises made and kept, echoing in her mind—chilling commitments to destroy her younger children from her marriage to Jim, her last refuge of innocence.

In this post-op recovery unit of the hospital, while most patients still slept, Hope heard the distant melodies of '80s alternative music playing at the nurse's station. When the fluorescent light behind her bed flickered, a cold pulse matching the erratic beat of her heart surged through her. The sterile air thickened as the smell of antiseptic morphed in her memory, becoming the scent of baby oil. No—*Corbin's* baby oil. Involuntarily, she gasped for air, and her stomach twisted violently.

The nights came rushing back.

His hands still slick with oil, the same scent clung to her flesh that seared with pain and her own blood after he was finished with her and left their bed. She remembered lying still, pretending it didn't hurt, pretending she could detach from her body. But his smell never let her escape.

A tear slipped down her cheek. She swiped it away as if it were a weakness she couldn't afford.

Her coccyx throbbed, a newly awakened reminder of the years Corbin had slammed her into walls and floors, his calculated strikes sparing visible damage but wreaking internal havoc. As the pain radiated through her back and right leg, a new song, *The Day of Reckoning* by Warren Heyns, played, and she thought grimly: *This pain I can manage. The echoes of what he did to leave me and my family this way require more... more than I can bear alone.*

The flicker of the lights pulsed again, snapping her out of the sterile present and hurling her backward in time. She remembered the last time she saw a light tremble like that. She had been pinned beneath Corbin's weight, his hand pressed against her throat, gasping for air, her head slamming against the tile floor. She remembered the lightbulb above them flickering before everything went black.

She shivered, her body reacting instinctively to the buried memory trying to resurface. She wasn't ready to confront it. Not yet.

The beige patterned curtain opened quietly, and the shuffle of Nurse Wendy's pale sneakers interrupted Hope's spiraling thoughts. Wendy's presence offered a small comfort against the hospital's sterile chill.

"Good to see you awake, Hope," Wendy said gently, pulling up a chair beside the bed. "You seem deep in thought."

Hope hesitated, grasped the solid metal frame of the bed, and took a long breath. She exhaled slowly, then whispered, "Wendy, I need you to listen."

Wendy's brow furrowed as she leaned in, sensing the gravity of Hope's tone. "I'm here. What's going on?"

Hope gripped the cool metal tightly, her knuckles turning white. "Every time I come here, I check the box on the intake forms—the one that asks if someone is hurting me. I always check 'yes.' But no one asks me about it."

Hope hesitated, her breath catching in her throat. Saying it aloud felt like ripping open wounds she'd worked so hard to suture in silence. She braced herself for disbelief, for indifference, for the same systemic shrug she'd known all too well.

Wendy's eyes softened with guilt. "I'm so sorry, Hope. I had no idea."

"Corbin didn't just hurt me," Hope said, her voice trembling but resolute. "He broke me. And when I finally escaped, the system handed my children back to him. Over and over again. He hurt them in ways..." Her voice trailed off before finding itself again. "When I lost them, I lost everyone left. And now Jim..." She struggled to put the inexplicable into words.

Wendy reached for her hand, her grip firm and steady. "Tell me everything."

Hope's words poured out like a flood, years of pain unleashed. She spoke of Corbin's abuse, the suffocating indoctrination of the church, and the legal system's betrayal from Corbin up to the present—now Corbin's ripples found her oldest children—and Jim.

She described the night she found the note tucked into Corbin's coat pocket, written in strong male handwriting that wasn't hers. *"Last night was unforgettable,"* it read. When she confronted him, he unleashed a storm of truth-twisting and blame-shifting called gaslighting.

"You're paranoid, Hope. You've always been insecure. That's the real problem. If you don't fix it, then our Forever Union will be forever awful," Corbin had pressed her before he took a shower, his voice fading under the sound of running water.

She had believed him, burying her gut instinct once again.

"Jemma and Fowley became worse than him," she choked out. "They're not my children anymore, Wendy; not since he got custody. They're his soldiers. Their identities overflow as appendages of Corbin—characters who involuntarily ooze mind games mixed with patience, forethought, and malice. They are simply two ticking time bombs waiting to explode, combined with their erratic, rageful outbursts free from consequences. They've promised to destroy my younger ones and everyone they will ever know, and they will, if I can't find a way to keep us together and safe. Jemma and Fowley are worse than the dad who raised them. They learned, as their dad has done to me, that it is a more insidious form of injury to harm my loved ones than to harm me directly."

Wendy involuntarily shuddered. "Isn't there anyone who can help? Family? Friends?"

"No one," Hope replied. "My dad passed away, as did my mom, so I have no family left. Our youngest children are understandably not okay with going back to Jim. I've tried shelters, but they say my older boys are 'triggers' because they're over twelve years old. We're turned away everywhere. As for Jim, he's supposed to be my husband, but he's not a protector. He's a High Priest in the church, and all he cares about is control and appearances. He sees our children as burdens, mistakes, and my manipulations to get pregnant, which is a blatant lie. He reminds me of that nearly every day, in front of every child who thinks that of themselves," Hope said, brushing a tear from her glowing cheek.

"How do children recover from a lifetime of being dismissed, told they don't belong, through actions and words by their own dad?"

Wendy leaned forward, her eyes filled with sorrow and disbelief. "What do you mean?"

Hope laughed bitterly. "Jim isn't violent like Corbin. His abuse is quieter and insidious. He uses words, denying truth, manipulation, and indifference. He convinced me that our path and every problem in our marriage were my fault, that I had tricked him into marriage so I could have children after four doctors told me I was barren from an STD Corbin gave me when he cheated on me, even before we were married. Jim's voice remains a constant bark that our children are unwanted mistakes. That is his true self when we're in the privacy of our home; then he dismisses his gut-wrenching, dagger-like words or insists that he never said them at all. Our younger children didn't want to get baptized. From age six, the twins, Molly and Matthew, said they'd been praying, and every time they prayed, they felt a bad feeling in their hearts— an inaudible "No." Despite my fears that I had somehow failed them as a mother, the three of us decided that age eight was just a number and that they should keep praying to see what the Lord guided them to do. That way, if and when they were baptized, it would only be in response to their prayers to obey their Heavenly Father, not any earthly parent. So the years passed, and we were not concerned about it. Several other children their age in their class didn't end up getting baptized. However, on the Sunday before Matthew and Molly's eighth birthdays, both still received a "No" when they prayed earnestly about being baptized in the Mormon church, now called 'The Church of Jesus Christ of Latter-day Saints.' Each one prayed separately and felt sick gut feelings about the Book of Mormon. But on that fateful morning, a different bishop than Jim cornered them in his office without me or Jim there, enticing them with chocolate 'for a talk,' alone together. He insisted that if they were not both baptized by their dad the very next Sunday, they would never see Jesus Christ, their Heavenly Father, or their present or future loved ones in eternity, and would suffer alone for eternity, stricken from all memories of their other relatives who were baptized. Terror tactics! There is no 'Hell' or even a 'Heaven' in Mormonism. 'Outer Darkness' is their version of 'Hell,' reserved only for people like us who dare to leave 'The One True Church,' 'Latter-day Saints' or Mormonism. Different brand names, same store," Hope attempted humor.

"Wendy, I was outraged when I learned just months ago, years later, once they were able to safely verbalize what happened, but Jim just rationalized and brushed it aside, even defending the other bishop. I am still not sure if he knew about that meeting beforehand, and I never will. That's the kind of dad and husband Jim is to them. He doesn't hit, but he wounds just the same, and maybe deeper, with soul-searing words worse than any other person has ever manipulated me with. And I'm an adult. What must it be like for them as children?"

In the stillness after her words, Hope stared at the ceiling. "Sometimes I wonder," she whispered, "if every heartbeat is just a call for justice. Is it the silence that lives between agony, desperation, and hope?"

Wendy's hands trembled as she absorbed Hope's reality. "This isn't right," she whispered.

Hope's laugh was hollow. "Tell that to the judges who let Corbin legally kidnap my children and gave him my Social Security Dependents' monetary benefits that would sure help me with the last seven. Tell that to the Social Security Administration that gave Corbin money meant for Jemma and Fowley after he was the one who intentionally inflicted the injuries that left me disabled. And tell that to whatever agency views the 'Church of Jesus Christ of Latter-day Saints' as a religion of any kind, and not just a political and multi-billion dollar corporate organization or coup led by co- perpetrators of crimes against my children, that needs their corporate veil pierced and religious tax-exempt status dismantled for the crimes they co- conspire in, help to cover up, and for hijacking the very name and nature of any Biblical Jesus Christ."

Wendy wiped a tear from her cheek. "What do you need from me, Hope? How can I help?"

"Nurse Wendy, you ask what to do?" Hope replied. "I will tell you the same thing an advocate told me. He said, 'Hope, sorry, but this is not your story. This is not uncommon. Your story and your children's is simply normal for at least one in every three women in the USA and across the world like you, and likely more than one in seven men, because reporting being beaten without bruises carries some shame for a good man of any age.' The advocate told me something like, 'Hope, you are going to feel uncomfortable speaking out and telling your story. Tell the people you know best because it is likely happening to others they know. Tell others that this isn't about ME, but about THEM. Wendy, your children and their friends, your grandchildren, your colleagues at work, your friends, even your friends at church—one in three women is a lot of women and their children, and this epidemic is getting worse, not better,' he told me. Who knew that he was a victim/survivor as a child, like my boys?"

Hope's voice grew hushed as she continued, "Nurse Wendy, in all the legal digging I have done to try to pull us out and into safety, I have only found one place in this entire world that has enacted legislation to protect legally established victims of domestic violence from further injuries through the courts and by third parties, like 'The Church of Jesus Christ of Latter-day Saints,' who dismissed and normalized Corbin's actions. This is the missing piece of legislation that would have saved victims like my own first living children whom Corbin had injured, too, from being twisted into our perpetrator's likeness and his own rippled appendages—worse than their dad ever was.

And you know what? This one place I found enacted these protective pieces of legislation amidst all other government shutdowns and simultaneously saved who knows how much money by preventing established perpetrators from misusing the family court, so that those misallocated millions in local government funds would be funneled into actually helping battered mothers and their children heal and get back on their feet. This one place is ending the cycle of abuse that comes from children experiencing their torturer wielding power in relationships and planting seeds within the children to replicate life-endangering and inhumane behavior for more generations. They cut off the head once there is a hearing and conviction of domestic assault against the mother or the children. Not always the women are victims, but most often."

Hope rushed on, "Nurse Wendy, if this one legislature could enact these protective provisions during the huge global shutdown and governmental gridlock of COVID, then why not now, nationally, statewide, countywide, and locally? Internationally? Why not NOW?"

Hope continued before her nurse and friend had to go tend to her other patients, when she'd have no one else to share these complete parts of her story with, who would believe her and know some way to help her and her family.

"Wendy, an advocate, told me something that shook me to the core. She said, 'Hope, find those people who are willing to be the ones who act on your family's behalf instead of just watching from the sidelines. Ask everyone to refer you to others they know, even if they can't help you directly. Keep digging. Keep telling and asking, and don't stop. Ask all the people you uniquely know to share your story with others in their lives who they alone uniquely know, and for them to share with others whom only they uniquely

know, and so on. In doing this, eventually, others who were once in a similar situation to those who injured you, like Corbin did, and had children like Jemma and Fowley, who were raised by the system to have no remorse or consequences, will empathize. Even if it is just so they don't have to experience a future filled with children who have become like the truly alienated, not estranged, adults that your Jemma and Fowley are today. Eventually, Hope, you will find those willing to help who have had enough and demand a better life, not just for your family, but for the billions of families like yours, and worse.'" Hope recalled, her body and mind too mangled to carry this message alone.

"I'm sorry," Hope stammered. "You asked what to do? Is this too much?"

Hope had always seen Wendy as kind, but not the type to get deeply involved. Yet something in her nurse's trembling hands indicated this was different.

After a silent moment, Nurse Wendy, tears involuntarily welling up in her sable eyes, pressed Hope's hand and whispered firmly, in shared determination for her patient and friend, "What am I to do, Hope? This can't be happening. I know you! Your babies. What am I to do to help you?" she queried, shaken, her strong hands of service now trembling.

Hope paused, in search of clear words, before she softly responded, holding her nurse's hand to steady it with her own courage. She whispered back with equal but calm resolve, "Tell others, Wendy. Raise your voice with mine, too, okay? People need to know what's happening because nobody seems to be listening to me alone or to others like me in the groups I attend."

"By the way, did you know they put Domestic Violence Awareness Month in the same month as Breast Cancer Awareness? I marvel sometimes at not knowing if breast cancer destroys 1 in 3 women's lives or has the same impact on 1 in 7 men. Yes, encourage your staff and anyone else you know who has ears to hear to keep wearing their pink ribbons, but make sure to begin wearing purple ribbons for me, for your loved ones, for friends, and for all our children and our nation impacted by domestic abuse or war crimes, right along with their pink bows for breast cancer throughout October."

Hope's excitement at being listened to and heard for the first time since... she stopped herself to just feel the present moment as gratitude and validation glowed through her physical and unfathomable spiritual and mental anguish.

After she spoke with Nurse Wendy, Hope saw the shift in her—the nurse's resolve had solidified, her commitment clear.

"I am taking this to our staff meeting tomorrow, Hope. Everyone here has known you since before you married Jim. I am with you, and I know the staff here will back you up, too. Would you be willing to write down your concerns to provide us with that protective legislation that will stop this from happening here or again?"

Before Hope had time to thank Wendy and locate the copies of the legislative acts she knew needed to be passed nationally and locally as only a beginning, the door creaked open again, and Hope's heart froze. But it wasn't Jim. It was Mr. and Mrs. Gideon, the kind couple who had taken a shine to Hope and her children. Paul Gideon carried a makeshift banner they'd brought from home, and Amy held young Sammy's hand, her warm smile lighting up the room.

"We brought the kids in," Amy said softly. "They were excited to see you."

Hope's children rushed in, their laughter filling the now bloodied room with warmth and light. She hugged each of them tightly, savoring their time together.

Holding her family close, for just a moment, she felt the contrast between her youngest son's innocence and the corruption she had grown to witness unfolding in Jemma and Fowley as they grew older. In these little arms of Samuel and each of her other children, Hope embraced parts of herself that Corbin or Jim hadn't stolen yet. Her children's laughter and innocence weren't just comforting—they were reminders of everything she was living, fighting, and worth dying to protect.

Hope's brood clamored around her bed, sharing stories about their stay with the Gideons and their extended family. Her children passed their mom handmade "Get Well Soon!" cards, and letters written with their personal thoughts, poems, and pictures from the older five. This was a joyful, carefree, fleeting moment for Hope. She laughed with them as they exchanged hugs and giggles. Hope pushed the pain aside—she was accustomed to this coping. Her children needed strength, and she couldn't let them see anything else in her. She delighted in each one of them, and they in her. Thanking Amy and Mr. Gideon and their family, Hope laughed aloud, "Oh, what miracles we are! To have each other, and you two who are more like my family than friends!"

As the Gideons stood by the door, Hope felt a glimmer of promised life pierce through her fear. But as she held her youngest child, Sammy, closer, she couldn't shake the nagging thought: *What if Jim is able to take all of them, as Corbin did with...?* Her heart raced, but she forced herself to breathe and to forget in the moment.

Author's Note

As you've read Hope's story, time hasn't paused. Somewhere—right now—another woman or child is enduring what she has. The statistics are not distant or abstract:

- **1 in 3 women**

- **1 in 7 men**

are impacted by domestic abuse.

These are your friends, your colleagues, your loved ones. Maybe even you.

And yet, their suffering is so often dismissed, hidden behind smiles and silence.

Hope's story is not unique—it's tragically normal.

What makes her different is not what she survived, but that she's telling it. Loudly. For those who can't.

It's time to act.

Not tomorrow. Not when it happens closer to home. Now. Start conversations.

Ask questions.

Stop assuming silence means safety.

Push for **legislation** that protects against coercive control, abusive litigation, and push back against the manipulation of systems meant to provide justice to victims rather than dismissal to the victimizers; put an end to wipe-the- slate-clean laws to shield perpetrators and obscenely short statutes of limitation. Demand repayment from perpetrators like Corbin back to their victims through the Social Security Administration when they are awarded dependents' monetary benefits for disabilities that they cause; as was Hope's circumstance.

Demand accountability, transparency, and mandated education— From religious institutions.

From courts.

From every official who allows this cycle to continue. From the perpetrators themselves.

Say STOP—NOW.

If we don't speak up, who will protect the next Hope? Her children? Yours?

Please:

Wear the purple ribbon. Raise your voice.

Refuse to look away.

Chapter 3

The Keeping: 1989

Hope's husband, Corbin, was dressed in the best suit Hope's six-figure salary could buy him as he opened the imposing brass door to the Latter Day Saint or Mormon Temple, engraved with six

symbols that Hope could not understand. Etched words cried out from high above the doorframe, "All Holiness to The Lord." No one had fully prepared her for this day. Her fingers trembled slightly as she smoothed her skirt— every step forward felt like stepping off a cliff in a dream.

"What is sacred and most holy to our Heavenly Father and our risen Savior remains in His Holy Temple," their leaders had said. "No one may speak of such things outside those hallowed walls. These delicate matters are sacred— not secret." In other words, whatever happens in the Temple stays in the Temple—even between members.

Upon their entry, Hope and Corbin lined up behind other Latter-day Saints who held current temple recommends—certificates signed by both their bishop and stake presidency attesting to their worthiness to enter. Each woman wore a dress or skirt, and each man donned a suit and tie.

They waited as the silver-haired men in spotless white suits and shoes behind the mahogany entryway inspected their temple recommendations for the signatures of their bishop and the higher priesthood authorities in their stake presidencies.

Hope and Corbin were soon ushered behind the naturally dark-hued wood of the entryway desk, and as she turned the corner, the sight stole her breath. The space bloomed before her—white upon white, the kind of purity found in fairy tales, like the glare of snow under a high sun. The hush in the air pressed against her chest. She blinked, unsure if she should feel awe—or fear. Instinctively, Hope brushed aside any sense of doubt, as she'd been taught well.

Aside from patrons like her and Corbin who were just coming in or leaving after their duties, all Temple workers and attendees were garbed in immaculate downy clothing, garments as pristine and stark as freshly fallen snow. The luxurious and classic furnishings echoed this purity and divinity—the ideal image of the Saints.

What Hope did not know was how deeply this exemplary place, along with those who governed it, concealed secrets within its foundation and current folds. The seamless alabaster washed over each carefully placed furnishing and the attendees within the white-marbled exterior assured a cloak of sanctity, whispering promises of a higher plane.

Hope and Corbin were guided to different sections—one for the male priesthood holders, the other for the women, or Sisters of the flock.

As they separated, Corbin's hand slid down Hope's back and lingered briefly, his fingers grazing the curve of her hip. She froze, her skin prickling under his touch. His grip tightened for a moment, possessive and intrusive. Her breath stopped short, but she didn't dare move. Instead, she let herself detach, floating above the moment as if watching someone else endure it. *Not here.*

Not now. Just keep walking. The voices of the Sisters beckoned her forward, and she obeyed.

***

Hope was whisked into a room brimming with other women, many of whom were young brides. Like others in waiting, she and Corbin had been married before, the midday sun unable to slice through the stained glass windows of his Catholic church as it drizzled outside. He said rain was a good sign for a wedding. But Corbin and his friends from his military time had promised that this different marriage, "a Temple sealing in The One True Church on Earth, for Time and Eternity," was the only path to true salvation, the only truth in religion, and the only place to rightly raise their young family.

Hope's mind drifted back to her early conversations with the Elders—or their Senior Companion, a civilian physician like Corbin. It always seemed that whenever she had a doubt, the Sisterhood somehow knew. Within a day or two, there would be a knock at their door, and Hope would be visited by the Relief Society Presidency, a hierarchy of the brightest and most valiant women in their area's ward building, at the small rented house near the base where Corbin was employed. With each visit, the Sisters brought answers to her questions. Hope was unaware that her concerns were shared behind her back by the Elders—and the Sister Presidency brought meals or treats paired with logical reassurances to quell any doubts that had arisen in Hope the week before; like popping balloons of logic with symphony tickets and chocolate chips. Once it was shared that the absence of females in the church's scripture reflected a protective act, sparing a Heavenly Mother from suffering the same blasphemies endured by Heavenly Father and Christ. The following Sunday, a hymn referenced a Heavenly Mother—Hope had lacked an earthly maternal figure, and their answers seemed to click for her, as someone with no solid knowledge of the Bible to compare their answers to. Hope had fit right in with The Church of Jesus Christ of Latter-day Saints/Mormons. She was a young mother to Fowley and Jemma, like many others in the ward near Corbin's base. She had no vices—she didn't smoke, didn't drink, and had worked to eliminate her use of profanity after years in the corporate world, despite Corbin and his military surroundings. The Sisters reassured her that Corbin's tendencies of physically rageful outbursts toward her and their two young children would ease, just as some of their husbands had learned to come into line.

But Hope's uncertainty suddenly returned. Her steps slowed, even as others nudged her forward. Each corridor seemed to shrink, not leading to revelation but to erasure. She wasn't sure what she was becoming—or leaving behind. Once again, caught up by Sisters she'd never had but had secretly yearned for, Hope forgot the questions she might have formed long ago, before Corbin. She covered her mouth as she smiled, swept up in the excitement and hushed giggles of the Sisters celebrating her new life with them.

***

Alone, Hope was led to an ornate Bridal Room—elegant and cold, with another bride eagerly waiting behind her to change. The Matron's assistant, warm but distant, handed her a thin white cloth and instructed her to undress. Hope's fingers shook as she unclasped her bra, her breath stopping short as she removed the last of her clothing. The cloth draped over her body, offering the illusion of modesty. It was flimsy. Insufficient. She was a grown woman, a mother—and yet she'd never felt more vulnerable, more reduced. She sat, waiting. Her palms damp. Her knees locked tight together. Then came the rustle of fabric. The Temple worker's approach.

Hope's discomfort sharpened when a woman who appeared to be in her mid- eighties walked in. The woman in white bent over and began to utter memorized promises of cleansing, washing, and anointing as her gnarled fingers moved over Hope's bare skin, applying the consecrated oil in practiced motions.

Each touch burned into her memory like a brand. The oil smelled bland, but in Hope's mind, it transformed into the suffocating scent of the baby oil Corbin used to lather himself with before entering their bed at night. Her breath quickened, and suddenly, she wasn't in the temple anymore.

The oil slid over her skin, and her body betrayed her—heart racing, vision tunneling. Without warning, her mind slipped away. She was back in their dimly lit bedroom. After he was finished with her, Corbin slipped out of bed, his shadow stretching across the room as he dressed quickly. The floor creaked under his weight, and the front door clicked shut.

Where did he go? she had wondered, trying unsuccessfully to wash away an unusual pulsing of bloody, blinding white flashes of pain mixed with confusion.

When he returned the next morning, she tried to confront him. "Where were you?"

He stripped off his shirt and headed quickly for the shower. "You're imagining things," he countered, his voice calm and clipped. "You've always had trust issues, Hope. Maybe you should work on that."

Her throat tightened. She forced herself to return to the present, to the older woman's touch and the oil sliding down her skin. As the woman's fingers grazed her thigh, the sensation triggered another memory—one she wanted to bury.

Corbin's military knife. The blade had been cold against her leg, not out of anger but as part of a cruel game. "Remember, Baby Doll, what's mine is mine, and what's yours is MINE!" he had growled, his breath warm against her flesh.

Her heart pounded. The woman's fingers pressed on her collarbone, but all Hope felt was the weight of Corbin's forearm nearing her throat and the darkness to follow.

Don't cry out. Not in here.

Hope dug her fingernails into her palms. The ceremony ended.

***

Hope's head spun, and her stomach churned as she was ushered by a woman dressed from head to toe in alabaster white, subdued cloth, back to the Bridal Room. There, the Matron's Assistant lavished her with flattering words about the blessing of being purified for her Heavenly Father and her Priesthood holder and spouse, Corbin, who was so valiant.

Hope chose her simple yet lovely eyelet white cotton wedding dress, appropriate for the upcoming Temple endowment and sealing ceremonies.

Hope had long known that no female voice spoke with the same Divinely appointed stewardship and authority in the One True Church. The titles— Elder, High Priest, Patriarch, Prophet—were worn like armor by men deemed worthy in God's eyes. She pictured Corbin, basking in solemn vows of virtue and duty, while she sat alone in her starched white chair. Once outside the Bridal doorway, Corbin's bride, Hope, was met with warm embraces from friends who called her Sister, without discussing their shared experiences. Her Sister-friends eagerly ushered her to the front row, nestled within the brightly lit, downy hues of the Endowment Room. Hope was seated in the beige amphitheater of movie theater-like chairs, divided by an aisle. Her Sisters guided her to the very front left aisle seat, where she saw a frosted cushioned altar before her, with a piercing white thin tapestry behind it, and Corbin just across the aisle, beside his fellow Priesthood holders, colleagues, and friends from the medical profession or the base. Hope's head was still reeling as a Temple worker, serving as a proxy for Heavenly Father Himself, bade all patrons to maintain a silent, reverent tone while they heard and made their Holy Covenants with the Lord. The older gentleman, dressed in a fine white suit and tie with matching shoes like all other Temple keepers, slowed his words and repeated his stern admonishment. Hope trembled, unprepared and unable to think or act despite herself, as the male Priesthood proxy for Heavenly Father repeated, "If there is anyone here who is unable or unwilling to make these Sacred Covenants with the Lord right now, we ask you to leave the room."

"What am I promising to?" Hope's mind raced.

"A Covenant is a two-way promise with God; they taught me that," she thought, frantically scanning her row and listening to the ones behind her to see if anyone was moving, straining to hear the clink of the door latching after someone left. But no one got up.

"If I move, if I dare leave, I will not only jeopardize my relationships with these new women who act more like Sisters, but also Corbin!" she thought, not daring to turn her head, lest any doubt cross his mind. Before she could think further, the proxy for God continued the ceremony, along with his female helpmate, the Sister at the front of the room, who came to give Hope her signs and tokens, assisting her with shifting her sash and veil, and adjusting the Kelley green fig leaf apron that a Sister's mother had hand-sewn for her eternity with Corbin. Sister Young had created one just like her daughter's for Hope, her new Sister, sitting just down the aisle.

As the male proxy for God promised the shedding of blood if any sacred signs, tokens, or Covenants were shared by any of the Patrons in the House of the Lord, Hope repeated the giving sign of placing her finger to her neck, as if to slit it. At the same time, the room spun, and every fiber of her being knew there would be no turning back. Not now. Her mind raced, "I'm listening as if my life now and in eternity depends on it, yet every syllable I hear and parrot back burns like acid on my soul. How can I trust these words when my heart screams only for escape, for freedom?"

This brain-fried bride, in due submission, allowed herself to be led unknowingly, like a sacrificial lamb, by the female helpmate to request the counsel of the Lord through the luminous veil at the top of the stairs. There, she simply repeated the exact words whispered to her by the Sister Helpmate and was whisked behind the opaque bright veil into the highest room her gender and status would allow her: the Celestial Room engulfed Hope whole.

The inner sanctum of the temple stood as a shrine to opulence and engineered purity. Walls and furnishings glowed in pale tones that seemed untouched by time, kissed by what could only be described as celestial light. Bleached velvet chairs and matching sofas were arranged in deliberate symmetry across the Celestial Room, flanked by vases of muted floral arrangements. Above, crystal chandeliers hung like frozen rain, scattering light into soft rainbows that danced across the floor—refractions of a divinity carefully curated.

Each piece of furniture, carved from the finest wood and bleached to near perfection, radiated tranquil elegance. Not a trace of dust marred the surface. Every detail upheld the Church's image of purity—flawless, sacred, and deeply controlled.

Hope wondered how much the others knew—Elders Olson, Calland, Dickinson, and Wright. They moved through the temple with the ease of men whose power had never been questioned. Had they, too, turned their hearts away from sins as deep as Corbin's? Her stomach twisted, and her mind began to jar at the thought of others like her husband. Hope stopped short at the thought of Corbin's admonishment against comparisons.

Encouraged and redirected by Brother Wright, her new Sister's husband, in whispered voices, she was reminded to ponder the blessings she'd just received and to seek the Lord's presence, as "He is found tangibly residing in His Holy Temple; in no other place on Earth will you find Him closer than in this very Room."

Hope, having been cleansed separately from Corbin, never to speak of the ceremony, was now set apart as one of the few elect among her Heavenly Father's children. With the stern caution to "always mind your Priesthood, and your Eternal Salvation will follow," Hope allowed her mind to count the newfound blessings assured to her; she had been cleansed of her past. She closed her eyes and bowed to pray. Hope's mind wandered to the recesses of her past, her courtship with Corbin, their formerly brutal marriage, and their two children, whom she would soon be connected to by the Highest of Priests, the Temple Sealer, acknowledged by the Prophet and President Himself.

Enveloped in the purity and grandeur of the innermost sanctum of the Church of Jesus Christ of Latter-Day Saints, this Heavenly Father's and Christ's one dwelling place on Earth, Hope looked up at the vast chandeliers above her and felt the soft downy velvet cushioned armchair supporting her small frame. In this holiest place on Earth that her gender could ever afford her, in the One True Church of God, where she would soon be sealed to Corbin for Time and Eternity, unlike the vows they had exchanged with family, dearest friends, and Father Mathius in the stained-glass Saint-filled Catholic church six years earlier, Hope finished her musing on the past.

"Such bliss!" she exhaled deeply, thinking to herself, "that Corbin could actually change! That I am cleansed from my offensive ways! That with Jemma and Fowley we're an Eternal Family... From the Mouthpiece of God Himself. Oh, how different things are now!"

Author's Note

What you've just read is the calm before the storm—a carefully staged facade upheld by power and fear. As you sit with Hope's experience, ask yourself: Could you walk away if everything—your faith, family, salvation—hung in the balance? Coercive control, especially when wrapped in sacred language, with people born of government or religious power—or both—holding all the power and control, is real, insidious, and devastating. Let this chapter stir not just empathy, but action. Speak up. Seek truth. Join the movement for accountability, healing, and freedom—for Hope, and for those still trapped in silent terror masked as patriotism or whitewashed sacredness.

Chapter 4

The Purchasing:
Before 1984

Hope's mother was her first abuser—the one who scarred her mind and body long before she understood the meaning of "abuse." At 18, Hope managed to escape her mother's grasp and home,

driving across the country from their small suburban town near Boston to attend college in California, taking sightseeing excursions along the way in her sunny yellow punch buggy.

In Hope's junior year at university, she sustained injuries in a brutal car accident. A social worker urged her to claim herself as a ward of the state due to damage to her leg, but Hope insisted on working through her painful injuries, trusting in defiant faith that things would somehow improve. Having juggled up to four waitressing jobs to support herself through college, she was forced to stop attending university when her legs no longer worked. She was just 30 credits shy of completing her BA—about a year and a half.

Each morning, she awoke with pain, but the loss of her degree hurt more than her legs. College had been her escape, her path to independence—and now it was gone. Still, she refused to surrender.

When her casts came off, she moved in with a college friend and began working as a temp, where she could sit down, answer phones, and type. The pay was low, but as usual, Hope persevered despite her setbacks and found joy in her work. She told herself her situation was merely temporary; she would soon return to complete her degree after saving money through hard work and dedication. The God she knew from her father's upbringing existed outside the confines of any religion. In time, her father's Savior favored her with full restoration and healing in both legs, freeing her from pain and granting her full range of motion. Several years later, she could run again without even a limp.

During this time, a mutual acquaintance introduced Hope to a man named Corbin, who was a few years older. He appeared to be perfect. He took Hope to beachfront restaurants, opened doors for her, took her coat, and covered her with his when the night air grew chilly. Every Sunday, Corbin called his adoptive mother like clockwork.

Hope hadn't grown up with a litmus test for choosing a partner, but she had studied psychology and sociology, intending to become a forensic psychologist after completing her undergraduate degree. Her friends and classmates advised her to look for a man who treated his mother with respect and to gauge his relationship with her to determine how he would be as a husband. By this standard, Corbin seemed ideal; he certainly doted on his mother, despite her living many states away. He called her every Sunday afternoon, although Hope later recalled that Corbin's adoptive mother didn't say much in response to his monologues.

Corbin showcased Hope at U.S. military parties in his dress whites before his peers. He had served in an elite military unit, where he claimed to train operatives in psychological warfare. The only proof she had of his past was the present—the parties with "his men" and their wives and families, the stories he shared late at night, the proud displays of medals in his closet, and her life with him. Romanced by Corbin with candlelit dinners and public professions of love, surrounded by the wives of his unit's peers, Hope began to feel as if she had the family she had always wanted but lacked in her youth. She tried not to fall too fast, but every time he wrapped his dress coat around her shoulders, something inside her softened—a hunger she hadn't realized still existed.

The abuse from her mother had jaded any desire Hope had to unite in marriage. Yet this young, strong, vibrant woman connected with the wives and children within the secrecy of Corbin's unit. Her first jobs as a youth involved caring for children at the small church where she grew up. Naturally good with children, she enjoyed helping them while needing to make money to meet her daily needs unmet by her self-absorbed, black widow-like maternal figure. So when Hope began to form bonds with the wives and children who banded together during their husbands' deployments, it felt as if something she didn't know was missing from her heart was suddenly being healed.

This fleeting pseudo-family was short-lived after Corbin began pressuring Hope to move in with him, which she eventually did. Soon after they settled into their new living arrangement, Corbin began to sever the bonds she was forming with each friend by pointing out flaws in the character of each wife, which would ultimately strain Hope's budding relationships with those she was beginning to trust and rely on as her only extended family. He warned her about each friend in unsettling ways: one was 'supposedly' an untreated alcoholic, another was 'maybe' cheating on her husband. Hope tried to verify the facts, but every time she asked questions, she hit dead ends. A nagging feeling told her these stories were designed to keep her isolated, yet she couldn't find the proof to confront him. Thus,

Corbin effectively isolated Hope not only from the new friends she had just made through his unit but also from her longtime friends from high school, including those she had lived with after relocating for college to escape her mother's rageful physical outbursts and other forms of abuse.

Not long after his slow, subtle, and effective severance of her ties, Corbin shook Hope awake—hard. "Wake up! Wake up!" he yelled as he shook her right shoulder from his side of the bed. "I want to have kids, and they won't be bastards, so you either need to pack your things right now and get out of my apartment or marry me! What's it gonna be?!"

Hope, half-awake and half-asleep, was confused and trying to think. It was far past eleven at night, and nothing was open for business. She was using Corbin's car to get to and from work, and she didn't have one of her own. She tried to stall with logic, stammering about why they needed to decide right now and asking if they could wait, but Corbin wouldn't budge.

"I want kids, and they're not gonna be bastards, so you need to marry me or pack your things right now and leave. I don't care where you go. There is no future for us if you don't marry me. If that's how it's gonna be, then you have trust issues with me, and our relationship won't last anyway, Hope. So you either agree to marry me now or get the hell out!"

Hope's heart thundered against her ribs, searching for an escape route. She tried to recall if any place was open—a motel, a friend's couch—anything to avoid saying 'yes.' But no solution came. She thought to herself, "Okay, I have no choice but to say yes right now and then leave in the morning when places are open—I just won't come back."

The more Corbin repeated his ultimatum, the more her world shrank, until she finally caved with a trembling, reluctant 'yes.'

Corbin leapt out of bed and immediately called the one person with whom Hope had tried to sever all ties: her first abuser—her mother.

Hope involuntarily cried out, "No! Corbin, no! How did you even get her number?!"

Corbin fired back, "Surprise, baby! She's YOUR MOM! I flew out to meet her and her new fiancée. You're going to love this!"

Hope felt as if she had been shot in the gut.

"No! Corbin, why?! YOU KNOW HER? Why did you meet her? HOW? I WON'T get on that phone!" Hope felt the room and her world collapsing around her.

Corbin met her on purpose? WHY? How did he find her? Why did they meet? A lifetime of questions, doubts, fears, and betrayal swirled in Hope's mind, and she wanted to vomit when Corbin shoved the phone to her ear and mouth, hissing, "Talk to her, Hope! She IS your mother!"

After that phone call, it was done. Hope's fate was sealed.

Corbin and Hope's mother began planning the wedding at midnight, insisting it was "for the families," leading up to that awful and unchangeable day of ever after.

Corbin's colors emerged just weeks after their coerced arranged marriage, orchestrated by Hope's maternal perpetrator, in Corbin's church, surrounded by a few friends and family that Corbin had only just convinced Hope to cut ties with. He hand-addressed and mailed out the invitations on his new wife's behalf, along with his adopted family.

The wedding was over, but there was no honeymoon.

A work-worn Hope returned to their marital townhouse after her 12-hour shift, exhausted to the core. Before she could prepare dinner, as Corbin typically expected, he stopped her.

Hope had changed jobs to suit Corbin's wishes months earlier, taking a telemarketing position she detested. However, she learned about someone named Jesus from a colleague and began praying throughout her shifts, setting ambitious goals and praising this Jesus man-God for helping her achieve what she could not on her own. Eventually, Hope was promoted to supervisor, and when the daytime sales manager position opened, she was promoted again due to her diligent work—more answered prayers from her Jesus—to meet Corbin's insatiable demands for more than her money could provide. He had already begun to repeat his first laugh of many to come after they exchanged their wedding vows; "Baby doll, what's mine is mine, what's yours is MINE! Don't withhold anything from me—IT'S MINE!!! Hahahah!" He tracked her whereabouts and belongings like a territorial lion eager to claim more than his prey.

When Corbin stopped Hope that night from making dinner after she managed to get through the door, she had been at work since 6:30 that morning, and now it was around 6:30 in the evening. As she entered the dimly lit lower level and crossed the caramel-colored carpet into the aging galley kitchen, she felt mentally and physically drained. By this time, with her promotion, Hope's income far surpassed her co-workers' and Corbin's as well. Yet every dime, each paycheck, she dutifully handed directly to Corbin to manage, as he had deemed her "too irresponsible to handle money." She had lost the sensation of simply holding a solid, crinkled or crisp, yellowish- green U.S. dollar bill, or any silver or copper coins, or lined and signed checks.

Just before their very public and ostentatious Catholic wedding, Corbin had beaten Hope so severely that oozing welts formed, seeping blood; she could not sit down for nearly a week after failing to reconcile her checkbook because she bought some gum.

Before beating his fiancée with his thick leather belt, Corbin yelled at Hope in a way that left her mind so warped she curled up in a ball on the floor of his apartment, sobbing like an infant, unable to catch her breath. Corbin drilled identity-warping lies mixed with partial truths into her mind as steadily and relentlessly as a jackhammer. In those fleeting moments, Hope became Corbin's practice subject for his work trainees. Truly, she was his Mona Lisa, a living sculpture to showcase for his trainees in Special Ops like none before or after.

No one had reduced Hope to tears, except for the woman who raised her, Hope's first perpetrator, who used her tears against her—any crying was a sign of weakness and easy prey to exploit. In those brief moments, Corbin, without a touch but armed with a hurricane of scalpeled words, left his once- strong fiancée curled up, unable to remember much of what he had yelled, except that it broke her inside in ways she had never experienced before— not even by her mother.

After his tirade, Corbin knelt beside Hope on the deep blue carpet while her shoulders heaved with sobs. He began to stroke her long, wavy blonde hair, crooning softly in her ear, "Oh my baby doll, I didn't mean it. I just wanted to see how far I could push you. A friend of mine from high school and I used to do this. Baby doll, don't you see how very LUCKY you are to have me?" His words flowed slowly, caressing the living room as he continued to nuzzle her head on the blue carpet.

He soothed her, "I will teach you! You know what you did, not being good with money, was irresponsible, and someone, your husband, needs to teach you that lesson, right? Don't you want to learn and be smarter next time so we can be equally yoked, like it says?" Corbin's voice shifted, becoming sincere, feeling like warmed oil intended to mend Hope's shattered mind and spirit. He pulled her from the fire of his making and immersed her mind in the cooling pool his words crafted. However, his next actions, though equally sincere in retrospect, lacked any basic human kindness or the healing balm of his honeyed words, placing Hope in a tepid bath poised to slowly simmer and boil her alive.

Bewildered and shaken, Hope was still catching her breath as Corbin pulled her to her feet. He led her to his bedroom, sat down in his full-dress white uniform on the soft baby blue comforter, and laid Hope over his lap, lightly raising her skirt. With every lash of his thick leather belt, Hope was made to count, "1 thank you, Corbin, 2 thank you, Corbin, 3 thank you..."

She quickly learned that if she involuntarily cried out, whimpered, or made any noise, Corbin would softly repeat, "Hope, that is not being a good student. Not my baby doll. I know you can learn, but if you are unteachable, we start all over again. No crying, remember? You made the mistake, not me. I am just teaching you. You DO want to learn, right? So, we will have no more baby-ness, understood? Take your consequences without a noise except to thank your teacher. Now we have to start all over."

"A thing of gum?" the thought trailed aimlessly through Hope's shattered mind before Corbin's next lesson.

With that, Corbin's unyielding belt resumed until Hope inevitably winced, made a face, or yelped in pain, prompting the counting to restart at "1 thank you, Corbin, 2 thank you, Chief, 3 thank you, teacher, 4 thank you, Master, 5 thank you, my Lord..." until, for some unknown reason, Corbin stopped; perhaps he was tired of his game—who would ever know?

Corbin then assured Hope that she was now satisfactory, ready for the next part of her education. He moved her still-clothed body across his now midnight-blackened bedroom and used colored bungee cords to restrain her to his Bowflex. Hope heard him curse under his breath as he rummaged through the closet. His teeth ground audibly when he came up short—only two bungee cords. He found a ratchet strap used for cargo on the floor of his closet, normally used at work, and decided that would suffice. She sensed a dark frustration radiating from him, and her stomach twisted, dreading what he might do next. She couldn't help but notice how carefully he chose each phrase, his tone clipped and deliberate—like he was testing her reactions to each word. Tethered to his workout machine and enveloped by the darkness of the room, Hope was now quite literally trapped. Corbin commanded firmly, "You do not want to move until I get back to find out those consequences, do you? Nod yes or no." As Hope nodded yes, Corbin slammed the bedroom door, and she heard the front door shut; his dress whites stained with traces of blood from the welts he'd inflicted on her thighs. The bloodstains clung to his crisp uniform, which he would later discard, frustrated that her blood would not wash out.

After realizing the isolation of her situation, and what felt like an eternity since she first heard the apartment door close behind him, she finally wept. "What have I done?" she thought to herself. "Who treats another life this way and calls it love? I cannot MARRY anyone but him? What do I do??"

Corbin had mailed out invitations to Hope's former friends, her extended family, and all of his family and friends the previous day after choosing and paying for the wedding dress, claiming "so the families won't be burdened financially by our wedding, but blessed."

After the wedding that Hope neither wanted nor asked for, she returned from her shift as the day shift sales manager at her telemarketing job. Corbin stopped her in her tracks with just the tone of his voice. Seated in his usual place—his recliner—watching television, he stated flatly, in the same oddly emotionless tone he used during his marriage proposal:

"I don't have the money to pay for that wedding after all. I'm on call 24/7 with my unit, and they need me, so I can't get a second job. But I found one for you. It's circled in the newspaper on the table."

Corbin's tone made Hope freeze. Her muscles locked, and her breath caught in her throat. She wasn't sure if she wanted to run, scream, or simply disappear. None of those options felt viable.

Slowly, Hope approached the table and picked up the newspaper. Her stomach turned. She read the ad again in disbelief. "Escort service?" she whispered to herself. Fury burned beneath her fear, and she instinctively cried out, "NO! Corbin! I won't do it!"

"Come on, baby doll," he feigned a tight smile. "You'll just be on the phones...." But soon, his fake smile faded, and he exploded, his voice rising from his easy chair as he lowered his footrest. "Remember, Hope, the word 'NO' is not one we use in this house—not to me!"

"Corbin, PLEASE, NOT THIS!" Hope countered, backing away from him. "Corbin, this says it's an escort service! I am NOT DOING THIS! You, my husband, are telling me to do this? What kind of man does that?! Besides, I make enough money. I just got home. YOU get the second job. I didn't want to get married in the first place!"

Hope had hit a nerve. Corbin flew out of his chair, his face beet red with rage as he threw Hope against the eggshell-painted galley kitchen wall and pinned her with his forearm pressed hard against her throat. She could feel the pressure cutting off her airway, while the vein in his temple throbbed as his face grew redder.

As Hope's vision blurred and darkened, the last thing she heard was Corbin's rageful voice simmering, "You dare defy me?! ME?!" as spittle oozed from the corner of his mouth. Then Hope's world went black, and her body went limp.

***

Hope woke up on the burnt orange laminate of the kitchen floor against the cracked wall in the dark later that evening. The scent of the baby oil and body wash that Corbin used overpowered the air, and she thought she sensed his presence in the adjacent living room. Terrified and still, she lay lifeless, her mind fumbling over the events that unfolded after her twelve-hour shift. Suddenly, she remembered: an ESCORT service?! Hope struggled to comprehend Corbin's blue ink circling the ad for "Angels of Modeling and Escort Agency."

"I am Corbin's WIFE. Why would any man suggest or urge his own wife to work at such a place? What is going on?" Hope thought to herself, trying unsuccessfully not to make a noise. Corbin's figure rose swiftly from an old wooden chair between the kitchen and living room, and Hope's body involuntarily shuddered in terrified uncertainty about what would happen next. As the bright kitchen light flickered on, Corbin knelt beside her on the hard floor and ran his thick, calloused fingers through her disheveled hair.

"Are you okay?" Corbin asked with deep concern in his steady voice.

"You really took a tumble. I wish you would take your heels off when you get home from work. That could have been a nasty fall."

Hope's mind reeled, her veins filled with icy shards of terror as she witnessed Corbin fracturing and recreating a false narrative before her eyes—his first of many lies in their relationship. His expressions shifted, the hue in his eyes changed, as he forced himself to believe the lies he was crafting, until his version became the only truth, devoid of the now shattered realities known only to Hope and a seemingly silent God, absent in her time of need for a miracle.

Instinctively, Hope flinched away from his grasp, but Corbin's strong arms swept her off the floor into a menacing embrace that felt inescapable.

"I love you, my baby doll. Remember that I will never let anything happen to you, right? I can't let you go until you tell me that you remember how I've always kept you safe. Right?"

With no physical strength left to struggle, and her mind clouded by Corbin's deceptive retelling of recent events, Hope was stripped of her ability to fight back. Escape was impossible, and silence was no longer an option. She used the last coping mechanism available: she fawned, answering in ways meant only to survive, not reflecting her true self.

Hope knew that if she simply muttered "sure thing" or "okay," whatever Corbin did next would be even more painful—physically, mentally, or both. There was no telling if it would be worse than the first strangulation she'd endured or the years of others that followed.

So, Hope used one of Corbin's own phrases in her feigned response.

Her voice struggled to escape her lips. She wanted to scream, to run, to vanish—but none of that would save her. Instead, she thought of the only words that might keep her alive: "Absolutely, Corbin. You are right."

"Absolutely, Corbin. You are right," she said aloud, hoping to satisfy her assailant, imprisoner, and husband.

Corbin led Hope to the small sofa in the living room and pulled out the newspaper with the circled employment ad. He gushed,

"Baby doll, I'm so sorry about your fall. You REALLY worry me with those heels, working all day and on this carpet at home. But we need to figure out how to get you this job. After your fall, I called and spoke with the owners. They're a really sweet couple—a husband and wife. Anyway, they said they would hold the last interview for you tonight. You just need to get there by eleven so they can talk with you before they close at midnight."

At that comment, Hope's spirit somehow stirred. "Corbin, wait—we need to talk about this. No." Corbin replied with a mix of sweetness and venom,

"What's to talk about? Don't be a baby now. You'll just be answering the phones."

Hope objected, but Corbin countered by insulting her character, questioning her integrity and resolve to "make and keep loyal covenants in our marriage."

"No, Corbin, that's not it. I will not work for an escort service, even to answer their phones. It's not right! Besides, your days at work are much shorter than mine. Why can't YOU work a second job?"

Corbin whined again,

"Baby doll, MY UNIT NEEDS ME. Don't you get it? I'm on call 24/7 to support them. I CAN'T be working at night. What if I get called in? You don't KNOW what I do, and I can't tell anyone—and you know YOU CAN'T TELL either. We operate unofficially; only the U.S. President gives our directives. We never know when we'll get a call. Do you want us to go bankrupt from the wedding just to please the family? We can't ask for help, right?"

To that, Hope replied firmly, "Corbin, no—I am not going."

Growing agitated, Corbin stood up, his tall and muscular frame overshadowing her smaller one. He looked back over his shoulder at her with a look she now recognized too well and said firmly,

"Yes, Hope, you ARE going—and I will drive."

Turning his back as he picked up his keys, Corbin added before spinning back around to bring his wife to their second car—purchased with Hope's money—

"Besides, if you don't like it after the interview, you can just not take the job. Deal?"

When Hope looked into Corbin's face and eyes, he resembled the man he had been when they first met—the one who opened doors for her, the one who still called his adoptive mother every Sunday, like clockwork. Throughout the interview, Hope paid little attention to anything except the time, exiting the Tudor-style building as quickly as she could. She opened the midnight-blue passenger car door and slid into the black cloth seat next to Corbin. He asked lightheartedly how everything went, and Hope happily responded,

"Wow, Corbin—it was awful! No way I'm going back in there. Thanks, but no thanks!"

The fact that Corbin didn't start the car or drive away was Hope's first clue. Decades later, she would ask herself,

"WHY, WHY didn't I just get OUT OF THE CAR before I went in? Or why didn't I run back up and call a cab or something after that? But NO! Dumb Hope! Well, that was, and still is, TRUE! I AM STILL just dumb Hope!!!"

Corbin then turned his face purposefully so that Hope would see his darkened expression highlighted by the parking lot lights as he let out a low, knowing laugh that rumbled from somewhere deep within him.

"Oh YES, you WILL go back, and you WILL work there, YOU GD FING BLOODY HORE!!! You WENT IN! I have it right here on my camera!!! You DON'T go back and work THERE tomorrow and all the nights after until I'm satisfied, then I will call EVERYONE from our wedding— YOUR friends, ALL your family—and SHOW THEM what a GD FING BLOODY HORE YOU ALREADY ARE!!!"

His deep, low rumble turned into a roaring, evil laugh that tethered Hope to him in terror of a false character dismantling through countless impending strangulations when he nearly killed her; all to protect this secret. Each time Corbin would say just the right word in public and in private, Hope remembered his promise.

Hope's character assassination and identity heisting that Corbin promised— not threatened—had only just begun. Every career advancement for Hope added to his leverage and unmatched power over her.

"I was strong before Corbin... I only answered the phones. Why did I stay?"

Hope would recall decades later, to only her closest advocates, her voice trailing off at the character decimation and lifetimes of her indescribable losses and irreplaceable decades of brain-blendering heists.

Author's Note

Strangulation kills. According to The Training Institute on Strangulation Prevention, half of domestic violence victims show no visible injuries, yet strangled survivors face a 750% higher risk of murder. Few perpetrators face prosecution. Corbin's ruthless isolation, physical assault, and rewriting of history demonstrate how quickly abuse escalates when no one intervenes. If someone had stepped in sooner, Hope's story might have ended differently. You can press for stricter prosecution and more rigorous training—visit **allianceforhope.com** to find out how. Please share this message to **save** a life.

From the outside looking in, Hope had it all together.

Who in your life has a lethal secret they're too terrified to tell?

Chapter 5

Mr. Magic: Twenty Years, 7 Months Ago

In the expansive living room of the new home that Corbin had pressured Hope into purchasing—funded by the next promotion she had earned through hard work, prayers, and grace alone—Hope sat at Corbin's cluttered desk, dutifully typing the surgical school papers he demanded of her.

After her long hours at work, she was weary, and thoughts of the other sister moms who stayed home to raise their rosy-cheeked children swelled within her. How she longed to stay home and raise her little ones like the other mothers she knew. Hope's heart sighed and sank. She knew it was envy and reminded herself to let it go. She did not bemoan her sisters, but there was a tinge of jealousy she needed to pluck from her heart to fully release it—their slow mornings, sticky fingers, lullabies to their babies instead of deadlines at work, and maybe more to their husbands. But she reminded herself again that wanting what others had was selfish. Her Priesthood leaders admonished it publicly. Corbin only echoed their truths.

She dimmed the room's lighting before setting about her task, hoping to calm her children—and, prayerfully, Corbin. Jemma, now a toddler, played quietly on the carpet, occasionally glancing at her mother with wide eyes full of silent curiosity. The smell of warmed milk from Fowley's bottle lingered faintly in the air, mixing with the vanilla-scented fabric softener she used on her children's clothes. It was a gentle, clean scent that should have been comforting, but tonight, it clung to her like a suffocating mist, reminding her of everything she was failing to protect. The clicking of keys was faint, nearly drowned by the persistent wails from Fowley's bassinet. Hope held her breath involuntarily as Corbin's keys signaled his entrance into their townhouse. Outsiders called him "Mr. Magic" as an endearment, yet every kind word or gesture oozed with the venom of his control and the intentional chaos he inflicted upon his wife and young children.

Hope's fingers moved slower than they used to, struggling to keep pace with the thoughts racing through her mind. Her hands hovered above the keyboard, sluggish and detached. Sometimes, they trembled without warning.

She knew she wasn't as fast as before; her coordination was slightly off, leading to mistakes she had to correct before continuing. It didn't escape her that she couldn't type as fluidly as she once had—her hands felt disconnected from her mind. She didn't know the full extent of the damage caused by Corbin's previous assaults and strangulations, but the tremors in her fingers and the aching tension behind her eyes hinted at something more than fatigue.

Her mind drifted briefly to the years before Corbin introduced her to the Sisters in Mormonism, and before this year, when his physical outbursts seemed to worsen towards her and the children instead of improve.

At least now, she wasn't left wondering what she had said or done. Corbin was angry at being passed over for promotions at work by younger men without degrees, angry that he wasn't being fast-tracked the way he expected. "At least he's still enlisted while I try to help him out," Hope thought to herself. Corbin hadn't served in combat and had always told her that military marriages suffer. He warned her that he didn't want her to be widowed if he was ever deployed.

Hope sat at the roll-top desk, her fingers quietly tapping the keyboard while Baby Fowley's wails escalated, reverberating through the walls.

Corbin shouted from downstairs in their three-story townhouse, "Hope! Can you keep him quiet? Or do I need to do everything for you, as a mother, too?!"

The sharpness of his voice sent a jolt through Hope's body, but she quickly darted back, sweeping Fowley up in her left arm, cradling his wriggling body against her chest while continuing to type with her right hand. His face pressed against her shoulder, hot tears soaking through her blouse as his cries from colic reached a fever pitch. She had to slow down even more to correct her mistakes. "I'm doing my best, Corbin. This application essay will be finished soon, just as you asked. I'm sorry that the military didn't accept—" Hope stopped herself short, panicking over what she had almost said.

The silence that followed her incomplete sentence was deafening. She could hear the distant hum of the refrigerator and the tick of the wall clock, but Corbin's lack of response terrified her most. She knew the storm was coming.

His heavy footsteps thundered up the stairs, each step reverberating through the floorboards like an impending execution. His eyes flashed with rage as he burst into the room. "What did you say? What did you say, Hope? Tell me to my face!"

Hope's breath caught in her throat. Her heart stuttered. One wrong word could trigger the worst. She backpedaled and played a Corbin. "Oh, sweetheart, I was just saying how much the military will regret not having you once your papers are done. Here you go!" She swiftly rose, removing Corbin's application from the printer to place it in his gaze and hands, holding Fowley securely in her arms while instinctively moving away. Hope ducked quickly down the hall and into the nursery, closing the door behind her to muffle the infant's screams. She silently prayed as she soothed her son with soft speech in her cradled arms, pacing and gently rocking him across the floor. She reached for the warming milk she had prepared for her infant son's comfort, hoping that Corbin would be satisfied while inspecting her work on his post-doctoral surgical school entrance essay long enough for her to soothe and feed her colicky son.

Corbin stood in the doorway to the upstairs den, reading the essay. His breathing slowed as his lips curled into a smug grin.

"Oh, my baby doll," he nodded slowly as he read her words. "This is good—really good. They're gonna eat it up, every last word! Did you finish my applications? Where in God's name are they?"

Looking around and seeing no sign of Hope but hearing the piercing wails of his wife's other priority, Corbin's furious rage invaded Fowley's safe haven and burst through the nursery door. He shoved Hope out of the way and against the wall opposite the crib, the bottle and her son just beyond her reach.

After Corbin stormed in, the faint scent of baby powder and Fowley's milk hung in the air, but neither offered comfort. Instead, the nursery seemed to shrink under the weight of his presence. The once-soft scents were now tainted by the smell of oppressive body wash and cologne, tinged with baby oil that didn't belong—sharp, overpowering, and inescapable. Corbin's breathing quickened as his gaze fell on the blue-and-white plastic baby rocker, the one Hope had cherished as a surprise baby shower gift from her colleagues at the online advertising agency before Jemma's birth. His expression twisted with disdain as his son's wails reached a different octave.

"This G-damn thing again? I told you it's useless!" he thundered, as he grabbed Hope's armful of infant and dumped their son, Fowley, roughly into the crib. The baby gasped, his small body curling instinctively away as he let out a shattering scream.

"Corbin! No! He's just an infant; you can't just do that to him!" Hope cried out, her voice trembling as she tried to push past him. But Corbin shoved Hope hard, hurling her slight frame against the wall where her body repelled her, leaving her crumpled on the hardwood laminate flooring near the pastel animal-patterned throw rug next to Fowley's crib.

Corbin lifted the fabric-covered baby rocker from Hope's friends above his head and hurled it down the hallway. The plastic legs scraped against the floor with a screech before it tumbled down the staircase, landing at the bottom with a loud crash. Hope flinched as she heard the sound of shattering plastic echo through the house, grateful it wasn't her son.

"Fking Fowley! Goddamned fking Fowley!! Shut the fk up!!"

Corbin slammed his fist near where Fowley's head lay in his crib, freezing Hope's heart as she made her way up from the floor. BAM! BAM! Another punch. The baby recoiled at the fist slams next to his head; it was sized not much larger than Corbin's fists. Fowley's shrieks grew louder, shattering the air and filling the room with a sound that seemed to vibrate the very walls, his small face reddening to a hue like his father's. Hope's chest clenched. She tasted copper; her body stretched out to find her son while her mind raced in terror and her spine screamed in sharp pain.

"Corbin, he's just a baby," she managed to say. "Just an infant. Please, let me take him. He will calm down if I can hold—"

Corbin snapped, "No, Hope! He is fine! He only needs to learn discipline, just like everyone else in this outstanding family of mine! Mind your Priesthood, Hope! Or don't you remember what the Bishopric warned you about?"

Hope reached for the infant in the crib again, tears streaming down her face, but Corbin's grip on her upper arm was firm and merciless. His fingers dug into her skin, leaving behind a punctuated ache of unwelcome familiarity, without a mark on her flesh.

"This isn't love, Corbin," she dared to whisper. "Whatever you think you're teaching, it's not love."

Corbin's expression shifted as he loosened his grip, his breathing steadying as his son's could not. His voice lowered to an unsettling calm, as if the outburst had never happened. "Of course, it's love, my baby doll. Everything I do is for you, for us, Hope. We're a Forever Family, right? This is all for you. Remember that when you're finishing my applications that are not on time but now past due. Tick-tock. The world doesn't stop spinning for anyone, Hope. Do you think you're so special? No; spoiled is more like it. How do you think this makes ME feel? I only wanted some peace for us both tonight. Now look at what you've done to ruin it!"

An unsettling calm washed over his countenance before Corbin turned on his heel. As he spun casually to leave the nursery, he hurled the $1,400 smartphone against the wall near Hope's face, the one he had pressured her into purchasing for him, knocking a baby picture off the wall as he left the room. The phone was useless, the screen cracked, and the framed collage of Fowley and Jemma's baby pictures shattered, glass raining down onto the carpet like scattered tears. Without looking back, Corbin headed down the stairs to watch television.

"You'll have to buy me a new phone tomorrow, Hope. You're lucky that wasn't my work phone. Your money, my money—what's mine is mine, what's yours is mine. Remember, my baby doll? You'd better clean up this mess on the staircase too. Somebody might trip and fall." His tone was light, almost sing-song.

Hope instinctively turned toward Fowley's crib and scooped up her sobbing son, cradling him tightly against her chest despite the sharp pain radiating through her neck and spine from where she had collided with the wall and floor. She rocked her son back and forth, sitting in the middle of the fragments on the floor, his tears soaking into the soft blanket. Hope's heart and mind froze when she noticed Jemma standing in the doorway, silently observing them before she walked calmly down the hall.

Her oldest child, Jemma, didn't say anything—she didn't need to. Her gaze was enough to tell Hope that she was learning, absorbing, internalizing.

At that moment, Hope didn't have the strength to stop it. She clung to Fowley, praying silently that her children would be shielded from this chaos repeating in their own lives. Regardless of her prayers, the seeds had already been planted.

After Fowley was calmed, fed, and fast asleep, Hope mustered her strength and carried herself down the hall to play with her daughter. Anticipating a rare moment of carefree time with her oldest child after a stressful day, Hope moved painfully but gratefully down the short hallway to play with her toddler. She found Jemma on the floor of her bedroom—the one she had let Jemma pick the color for, painted a dusty light pink just a few weekends prior. The scent of new paint still lingered.

Hope simply watched as Jemma worked busily, placing a doll's belt firmly across a rag doll, pressing the belt across its neck, yelling, "G-d fking hoar! Who do you think you are? You can't defy ME!" and other curses she had heard—curses that Hope realized, with a growing sense of dread, Jemma had absorbed from witnessing Corbin's repeated outbursts upon her mother.

Hope's knees buckled. The words—those exact words—had passed from Corbin's mouth just hours ago. Now they echoed from her young child. *"Oh Lord— from the mouth of my daughter?!?! Oh Lord—no!"*

"Jemma!" Hope cried out in alarm. "That is not okay! We don't use those words! You are hurting your dolly! Remember our only rule, Jem? We do not hurt others—not ourselves or our things, not with words and not with our bodies. You remember, right? Our only rule?"

Jemma didn't even turn to face her mother as she replied plainly, "I didn't hurt anything, Mommy. I love my dolly. Just like Daddy loves you."

Hope didn't bother with a time-out for her daughter. She returned to Fowley's now-quiet nursery, sat in the wooden rocker, and wept for the first time since that dreadful day before her Catholic wedding, stifling and muffling her panic-stricken tears. Just as on that long-ago day, there was nowhere and no one to turn to.

Hope's mind raced in terror for her children—not a thought about herself, but about what they were exposed to around Corbin, or what would happen when he decided she was of no more use. Would he simply press his hands against her throat for just a few more seconds or minutes needed to complete the task and upscale to an even younger wife and mother for their children?

Hope counted herself fortunate that Corbin seemed far too distracted by his own desires—watching television, spending hours on the computer in the living room, and working odd hours outside the home. He barely paid attention to their young children unless there was a party to showcase them at.

"Oh, Mr. Magical, how is it that you only act this way around us—around me? How magical you truly are, right?" Hope questioned herself again as bitter, bewildered, silent tears streamed down her cheeks in the shadows of the immaculate lemon-yellow nursery she had created as a haven for her newborn son. She wilted into the wooden rocker and buried her face in the blanket's soft fleece, worn from many washes, its softness the only thing left in her life that hadn't turned sharp—unlike the shattered glass and jagged words that could not be unheard from her four-year-old daughter's mouth. Hope wept in agonizing solitude as her innocent young son slept.

Author's Note

Strangulation is not just violence—it's a red flag for murder. Victims are **750% more likely to be killed** later. Half show **no visible injuries**. Nearly all know their abuser. Most victims are women. Most perpetrators are men. And in 50% of these cases, **children are watching**.

Children like Jemma don't just witness abuse—they absorb it. They imitate it. This is how the cycle continues.

Hope couldn't catch her breath—because she wasn't allowed to. Neither could her son or her daughter. The abuse wasn't just physical. It was psychological warfare: love bombing, gaslighting, isolation, control. There was no space to think, to plan, to ask for help. Her children learned from the one in power.

This is how **Complex PTSD** begins. Flashbacks, dissociation, silence. Victims—especially mothers and their children—often don't even know they're living in trauma until it's too late.

Trauma-informed therapy can be life-saving. But for many civilians, it's unavailable or unaffordable. For the military? It's a given. For survivors like Hope? It's out of reach.

This story is only fictionalized to protect the identities of pure truths—**many truths**. For many, like the real-life Jemma and Fowley, help is too late and never came. But for someone in your life, change might be possible.

Don't look away. Listen. Act. Persist.

Because someone, many, right now, still need your help.

Help that only—you—can give.

What if you don't lean away?

What if Now, you lean—

IN?

Chapter 6

The Bloody Hole:
Twenty Years, Nine Months Ago—Bleeding Into Present

Hope had confided in three of the wives of her Priesthood leaders about Corbin's rageful outbursts—how he directed his fury not only at her but also at their young children. The Bishop knew. So

did his President and the Counselors. They had even brought it before the Stake President. But the response was always the same: a haunting silence wrapped in smiles, a deafening dismissal cloaked in religious authority. Over time, their lack of action chipped away at Hope's reality until she began to lose sight of what was true. She later named it "The Bloody Hole"—a place where obvious truths disappeared for hours, days... even years.

Their response was as unforgiving as Corbin's wrath. The letter she received from the President/Prophet's office in Salt Lake was resolute and suffocating.

"What has already been Sealed for Time and Eternity cannot, will not be Un-Sealed, lest you, young Jemma, and Fowley be cast into Eternal Darkness. Where else would you go?"

The words pulsed through her like an electric shock, making her fingers tingle and her breath catch.

The letter trembled in her hand. "Sealed for Time and Eternity"—the words were more than doctrine. They were chains.

Suddenly, the scent of olive oil blurred with the colors and sounds from a 1970s movie on a large screen. She was no longer in her living room but walking the pristine halls of the temple, alternately sitting and standing as scenes shifted. The alabaster room and scattered chandeliers sparkled above her. After the movie stopped, she found herself in the Celestial Room. The hush, the reverence, the desk and Matron before the ceremonial washing room—it was all achingly perfect and swallowed her whole.

Then the flashback twisted. The hand of the temple worker slid beneath the cloth, oil dripping like unwanted truth. Hope flinched back into the present, gasping. She stared again at the immaculate white letterhead, its words as damning as the past they tried to sanctify.

With the letter in hand, Hope was jolted back to the present, sensing crimson on the cornerstone of the Church of Jesus Christ of Latter-day Saints/Mormon Temple's immaculate exterior—hidden stains on the very foundation, like the blood on Corbin's military dress whites. These tarnishes could not be erased or scrubbed clean, no matter how much outward sanctity or new Presidential/Prophetic revelation was proclaimed. Hope saw her marriage to Corbin anew, as a reflection in a Church of Jesus

Christ of Latter- day Saints/Mormon Temple mirror: outwardly perfect, but kept hostage in stifled isolation, walking on eggshells in mind-blending terror of what unknown infraction would set him off next, and Corbin's nightmarishly different actions when no one was there to bear witness to the truth.

Hope re-read the closing line once more, the words etched a chemical burn: "What has already been Sealed for Time and Eternity..." The rest blurred. She didn't need to read it again; it had already been burned into every glimmer of her soul.

Confused, her eyes scanned further down the page. Her many actions were dismissed, while Corbin's were exalted. Perhaps these were just expectations for every Church of Jesus Christ of Latter-day Saints/Mormon woman? There was no mention of her long hours at work, or her endless days as the sole caregiver to Jemma and Fowley, the only housekeeper, cook, peacemaker, and Corbin's supporter.

Acid rose in her throat as she remembered her hard work drafting just the right essay to secure her husband's choice of schools and the applications she completed that he merely chose and signed off on. Corbin turned down Stanford's acceptance letter, along with a slew of other highly ranked schools, to advance his career and pursue a degree in Medicine to become a Surgeon. His decision was swift and just in time, before he would have been deployed overseas to serve in action with the rest of his unit.

Instead, he accepted the one school within driving distance of the woman Hope had done everything possible to escape. He had physically forced the phone onto her face with her first narcissistic annihilator to seal their marriage and her fate. Hope dreaded the days and nights she'd agonized over that entrance essay and those applications for Corbin's gain and her own decimation.

Nearly twenty years ago, she had taken her sweet time weaving "throughout the countryside from Boston to California just to escape that woman's clutches, for what?" Hope wondered. She noticed a new hole in the plastered wall and the cracks around it, that had likely come from Corbin's fist, as she walked through the front door, and into the Boston brownstone she'd just purchased to further Corbin's educational aspirations.

No. Instead, Corbin had gleefully chosen the Ivy League University just a few minutes from the woman on Hope's birth certificate. Corbin's career change and his other upward moves ignited conversations between Corbin and the woman who had first crafted his wife's name into a curse; her mother.

Corbin and his mother-in-law's talks revolved around visits or "MeMa" time. Of course, she was too young at age 72 to be called "Grandma" or anything that made her sound so ancient. After all, what belonged to Hope was, by default, hers. Hope "owed her" for her "decades of ingratitude," "utter selfishness," and a slew of other adjectives that the Black Widow Wife of her three husbands past had branded upon her daughter long before her untimely conception and failed abortion, after an adulterous union that led to divorce and a new marriage, protected by a Court-Sealed Birth Certificate that shielded her mother's past. This had kept her from the truths of her birth and lineage that Hope's Court Order to access her original Birth Record had uncovered during her teenage years.

Hope shuddered involuntarily at the cold, intrusive memories of the one who called herself her mother and forced her mind back to the present.

The chilly New England cellar was full of boxes yet to be carried up and unpacked, but the essentials were there. They had just arrived a month ago, but Hope had been fortunate enough to secure a position before relocating from the outskirts of San Diego.

She had just returned home from work, juggling Fowley in one arm while Jemma tugged at her skirt. The house smelled of stale air and Corbin's body, with the faint hum of the refrigerator the only sound breaking the oppressive silence. Once, the scent of baby oil had evoked innocence and babysitting in her youth—now it sickened her. She would carry that revulsion with her until her last breath, along with the scent of Corbin's body washed in it, mixed with the fragrance of the wash he used that could never cleanse the mixture of him pressing over and upon her.

Corbin's voice filtered down the long hallway to the study as he spoke on the phone. Hope slowly climbed the stairs and set Fowley down. She slid off her heels and lay sideways on the bed to ease her aching back. Jemma hurried off to explore her new room, searching for her favorite toys that Hope had made certain to unpack first. Jemma's mom created a treasure map for her daughter to help her discover her toys and explore their new house, easing the pangs of relocating for them both.

As Hope reached for the bedroom phone to make a quick call of her own, the line connected her instead to Corbin's conversation.

"Does Hope know?" a voice spoke on the line.

Hope's fingers froze on the receiver, its smooth plastic suddenly slick with sweat. Her breath caught—this wasn't a crossed wire. It was Corbin. And someone else. She pressed the phone closer to her ear, her hand trembling.

"Have you been checked for STDs?" The voice became loud and clear. It was their first Bishop from California. But what was he talking about? A chill crept across her arms, raising goosebumps. Her pulse thudded in her neck, loud and hot. She didn't dare hang up.

"If you've given her something—AIDS, God forbid—it'll reflect badly on us, Corbin, especially after we've been covering the costs for your outside counseling. Honestly, you earn enough to handle these costs yourself, Brother Dekker." He paused, the rustling of papers filling the line.

"The discharge notes don't look good: predatory behavior, sadism, lack of remorse. Lifetime intervention is recommended, and even then, you're unlikely to be safe around Jemma and Fowley." The Bishop exhaled. "If she calls the police at all, we might not be able to protect you this time, Corbin. Understood?"

Hope's body locked. A cold chill spread from her spine to her fingertips as she pressed the receiver tighter to her ear. Her free hand covered her mouth. AIDS? STDs? Intervention? Jemma and Fowley? What was he talking about?

"No, Hope doesn't know," Corbin replied, his tone curt and controlled. "And none of you will tell her either. She's not calling any cop. She did it before in Cali, and I ripped the phone out of the wall before clearing up her misunderstanding.

Clearly, it was a misdial, and they left, just like she told them to," Corbin continued with ease, omitting the fact that the tip of his military knife was not pressed but touching that familiar part between her shoulder blades if she did not take back the reason for her 911 call.

There was a brief pause before the Bishop continued, joining in Hope's husband's guttural laugh, his mirth quickly turning lighthearted and dismissive in camaraderie.

"All right then, look, I've been on both sides of a disciplinary council, son. It's not so bad. Here I am, right? Your Bishop! Haha! Corbin, bud, you're turning 40 this year, aren't you? Just a midlife thing. It happens. The bonus is, you're in a new town, a new state, and a fresh start. New Bishop, too..."

Hope's mind fractured. *A midlife thing? The Bishop—THEIR Bishop knew?! The Church knew?!* Her husband had been with other men?! Not just once, not just by accident, but strings of them. Hundreds of them, if Corbin's admissions she was hearing were true. And she had never known?!

A chill crept over her skin, goosebumps rising as if her body anticipated the dread her mind had yet to process. Her heartbeat thudded in her ears, drowning out Corbin's voice for a moment. She gripped the phone tighter, her fingers slipping against the plastic as her chest tightened, each inhale a struggle. The air thickened with her mounting confusion, mixed with an odd sense of juxtaposed relief and terror. Covering the phone to muffle any sound, she waited for Corbin to hang up so she wouldn't be detected.

He tried to kill me last night, she thought, her eyes darting to the door. Her hand hovered over Fowley's chest, feeling the gentle rise and fall. She had to leave before Corbin made good on his promise.

Corbin hung up downstairs, unaware of her discovery, and so did Hope. She backed away from the phone as though it had burned her, her stomach wrenching up to her throat. Four months after her C-section with Fowley, two years after losing a stillborn son to Corbin's beatings, she pressed her hand against Fowley's shoulder as though to protect them both from the truth.

After overhearing the two-way conversation between her husband and their Bishop, the last shard of Hope's trust in anything or anyone shattered within her, reflecting splinters of her reality—the broken pieces of her life that once seemed whole now lay exposed for her psyche to absorb. She flinched, remembering her babies' mangled rocker that Corbin had tossed down the stairs at the house they'd just left, like the few tiny shards of broken glass from the baby pictures that Corbin knocked off the wall after smashing his phone against it near her face as if it were happening here and now in a new and different way. Each layer of the Bishop and Corbin's revelations splintered through her perceptions and forced forgetting, leaving sharp fragments of truth that cut deeper than she realized she had room left to endure.

Her legs wobbled, and she laid Fowley on his play rug while Hope stumbled into the bathroom, retching into the sink. No amount of vomiting would expel the swift truth from her system. She cupped water into her hands to swish around in her mouth, but still felt as if more was coming up, so she scrubbed her hands and splashed water on her face until the mirror blurred. The reflection staring back at her was hollow-eyed and broken. In just the past few weeks since the move, Corbin's outbursts had worsened, not improved. The blows came more frequently, and the strangulations lasted longer.

Hope mused momentarily, "Well, maybe all of this is just it. I can never please him because I will never be what he wants—another man." She reeled as she experienced an odd sort of relief, realizing that perhaps these relentless years of mind-bending, rageful outbursts upon her and their children were less about her and more about her husband's well-hidden alternative preferences. Last night, however, Corbin changed tactics and upped the ante.

Right now, he was downstairs either on the computer or watching television—or, suddenly, Hope thought, "Arranging his next date?" She quietly and quickly moved back into the bedroom to locate her diary from its hiding place and pulled out the Domestic Violence brochure she'd stashed weeks earlier while Jemma was at a drama class at the library, securing them in her purse and hiding them out of sight to read through later in the evening.

When she'd first picked it up, Hope had called after reading it, not knowing why. She was told that they could not and would not help her unless she was ready to permanently leave what they called her and her children's "perpetrator." Hope had resisted then, saying that she just "needed a break…to think things through," and was told to call back if she was ever ready. She tried to get a break. When Corbin's outbursts would begin, Hope calmly stated that they needed to go for a drive until he calmed down.

Despite everything, Hope's attempts to leave never stuck, not on the West Coast and not here either. This was another consistent pattern in their relationship. Hope would say she was going for a ride while Corbin cooled down, and he would inevitably follow her outside, pulling at Jemma and Fowley as if they were wishbones he could snap in half.

Young Jemma kicked back furiously, her small legs thrashing against Corbin's grip. Hope saw the fire in her daughter's eyes—raw, fierce, and unrelenting. It struck her with sudden clarity: Jemma wasn't just afraid. She was fighting—for herself, for her mother, and for her baby brother. That resistance, that spark—Hope felt it ignite something inside her, too.

Hope always returned inside the house, unable to leave her children with Corbin and unable to untangle them from his iron grip. These two were her reasons for leaving. It would be unthinkable to leave either behind with Corbin to be further harmed in her absence.

But after he suffocated her last night, something inside her had shifted. And it wasn't about the men their Bishop and Corbin had just spoken of. That, she would have to process later.

Her body still ached from the previous evening's "discipline." When he'd forced her onto the sofa, she thought she knew what to expect—but this time, he didn't grab her throat. He swirled her around in front of him, facing away, pinning her arms behind her and pressing her face into the soft cushions of the sofa, his full body on her head and torso. Her muffled screams were swallowed by the fabric. The more she struggled, the heavier his body became—like a stone slab crushing her chest and swallowing her mouth and nose as her movements faded. The smell of his body wash invaded her senses, burning her nostrils as darkness crept in. The room disintegrated into a blur of gray, then black, as oxygen slipped from her lungs.

"Daddy, stop! Daddy, don't!"

Jemma's voice pierced through the suffocating fog just before Hope's world went dark.

Hope's mind flickered with fragmented thoughts and jolted back into the present: *Jemma. Fowley! They need me! He's going to kill me next time! Or them!*

When she'd awoken from the black fog last night, her first breath had been a ragged gasp that scorched her throat. Jemma's small hands were shaking her mother.

"Mommy, wake up! Mommy, please wake up!"

Hope heard her daughter's desperate sobs and felt her tiny fingers and hands delivering forceful shoves upon her ribs and arms, saving her from what could have been their end. She heard Corbin cursing as he walked away down the hall. Even as if it were happening now, Hope could still feel Jemma's tiny fingers gripping her own, as if her daughter were holding her together as she awoke from what could have been worse than death for them both.

Suddenly, Hope was jolted back into the present, the day after his most recent attack, and into the stark new revelations of the moment as she heard Corbin's footsteps thudding closer and entering their bedroom doorway. Her stomach twisted with dread. Before she could step away, his hand clamped down on her arm, his fingers digging into her skin like hooks. He spun her around, forcing her to meet his gaze.

"What's with you today?" His breath reeked of cappuccino and dominance, his lips curling into something between a sneer and a smirk. Without waiting for an answer, he yanked her forward and crushed his mouth against hers, nearly stepping on Fowley underfoot, who had learned to scramble away as he crawled. Corbin's tongue invaded her mouth—hot, suffocating, as though he could devour her resistance and leave her hollow.

Hope's body went rigid, her breath caught in her throat. She couldn't pull away. His grip tightened around her waist, pinning her against him as her mind screamed for air. When she finally twisted her head to the side, he released her, but not before leaning close enough to whisper, "You are my woman, Hope. I ride 'em hard and put 'em away wet. Now you're good for nothing to me! Go sleep on the couch. And don't touch my things, or you'll regret it!"

"NOT the SOFA?!" Hope's mind raced as she replied weakly,

"Oh, Corbin, I just threw up." She swallowed hard, her voice barely above a whisper. "Please—just this once—could I have the bed?"

The words tasted dangerous. Asking for anything had consequences. But the couch felt like death, and she didn't think she could survive another night in its grasp.

"G-D Fing Hope! What's wrong with you?" Corbin's face twisted in disgust as he stepped back, wiping his mouth as if her presence left a stain. "You're gonna make me sick, too! Why didn't you say you had a cold?! Go sleep on the couch, and I'll take the bed," he snarled.

At his second mention of "the couch," Hope's mind spun back to the suffocation of last night. She shuddered as she responded in desperation.

"Corbin, please—just this once—could you take the guest room and let me sleep here? After all, this is where I've been, and my sickness along with me..."

The thought of either the sofa pillows or the piles of their shared bedroom pillows twisted her stomach further.

Corbin exhaled sharply, his face contorted. Annoyed, he shushed her, snapping,

"Don't touch my clothes or any of my things, or I'll know!"

Snatching his belongings, he stormed toward the guest bedroom and slammed the door behind him.

In the throes of horror, Hope found herself exhausted but unable to rest. She lay awake all night, tossing and turning in fear of Corbin returning to "accomplish his mission" and smothering her with the bed pillows that bore the weight of his scent. The room, now void of Jemma's presence, reminded her of his attempt to snuff out her life just 24 hours prior.

Bright and early the next morning, as Hope was dressing, Corbin swung the bedroom door open as if he'd forgotten his former disdain.

"Good morning, my forever wifey. What if I give you a massage later? You've been working so hard. You must feel horrible with that cold. I know the lymphatic pressure points, and that will help."

Every nerve in her body screamed. Corbin had never offered her kindness without an ulterior motive. His Special Ops knife lay unsheathed beneath his side of the mattress—always within reach. She could almost feel its cold steel tip pressing against her skin, forcing her into actions outside her will that she later found incapable of describing. Instinctively, she flinched when he reached for her.

His tone hardened instantly.

"Now, I've done nothing to deserve that treatment!" Corbin's eyes narrowed, his grip on her arm tightening to the point of pain.

Her mind raced. She had become adept at maneuvering around his traps, appeasing him with calm tones and loyalty.

"Corbin, I'm just waking up. You did nothing wrong. I just remembered I need to get groceries for the week and tomorrow's dinner. I'll be back soon."

She slipped by him through the bedroom door, fully dressed with her purse in hand, readying Jemma and Fowley for a car trip.

During the night, Hope had silently rushed to find the few important documents that the person at the other end of the local hotline on the pamphlet had urged her to bring weeks ago, placing them gently in her oversized purse along with five diapers.

"I'll pack some snacks for Jemma in the morning...I already have a pack of diaper wipes and bags in the car," she'd reassured herself the night before.

The once vibrant walls of the house, which Hope had done everything in her power to make into a new home pleasing to Corbin, now dulled, mirroring the fading light in Hope's eyes. The creaking floorboards echoed her fragility, each step a reminder of the instability beneath her as she packed up some snacks for Jemma and water for herself before heading out the door.

"We're off, Corbin. See you later," Hope hollered uncharacteristically into the house before shutting the side door behind her.

Hope buckled Jemma and Fowley into their respective car seats. As she slid into the driver's seat, she struggled to buckle herself as her hands trembled in foresight; the steering wheel felt cold and slippery under her palms, sweat beading on her forehead in the summer heat. Her breath came in shallow gasps, as though Corbin's hands were still wrapped around her throat. The bright morning sunlight was blinding, but she backed out of the driveway and put the midnight green-silver-flecked sedan in drive. Toward what, she didn't know. Her hands trembled against the steering wheel as she drove.

Her breath jumped as Jemma's laughter rang from the back seat. She left without bringing much, except for one of her journals with scribbles about a pamphlet she'd found in a bathroom stall for domestic violence victims. Hope had picked it up randomly, but in reading it, she'd found a voice to describe bits of her life. She packed only the essentials—not even a diaper bag—and headed as far away from the house—she'd bought at Corbin's insistence—as far as she could without stopping.

"Where am I even going? What do I tell Jemma?" Hope asked herself as she headed down the street.

"To wherever the voice on the pamphlet hotline tells you to go," Hope answered herself back.

She was leaving to keep her children safe, and this was the first time without a scene from Corbin.

This time was her first time in decades when she *could* leave. She wasn't coming back.

***

Author's Note

Every wound tells a story—and behind every scar is the promise of survival. But survival isn't just personal. It's political.

Research shows the most dangerous time for a battered woman is when she tries to leave. Separation increases the risk of being killed by 75%. Many abusers who commit homicide have made that threat before. Abusers like Corbin, for there is far more that remains unwritten about other ways he harmed Hope.

This is not just a story—it's truth: a mirror, a warning, and a call. If this chapter stirred something in you, act.

Reach out. Speak up. Demand stronger laws and protections.

Contact your legislators, your local officials, even the White House (www.whitehouse.gov/contact).

And if someone(s) you love came to mind while reading—gift them this book.

Your courage to act will likely save more than one victim's life.

Chapter 7

Mind-Sweeping:
Twenty Years Ago through
Ten Months Past

Hope still felt the raw gouge she later named The Bloody Hole, which Corbin had carved into her memory—an empty, throbbing space where certainty and instinct used to reside. She couldn't even trust the color of the sky, let alone the certainties that thundered past her like herds of purple stampeding elephants, unnoticed by anyone close to her or Corbin. The Bloody Hole was indeed contagious, affecting all third parties in common contact with Corbin, as well as his wife.

Somehow, Hope was guided to pick up a pamphlet describing domestic violence in a women's bathroom while changing Fowley's diaper, as they waited for Jemma's drama and art classes to finish, just weeks before leaving Corbin that morning. She dared not keep something like that on her, so she scrawled the listed phone numbers in the journal she had begun writing to track her sanity. She'd noticed Corbin's violence increasing and his blatant denials of what he'd done to her and their children—a term she would decades later learn was gaslighting.

When she drove to the outskirts of the small town where they were, she pulled over to a park and brought Jemma out to play while she nursed Fowley.

Every laugh from Jemma felt like a brief reprieve from the constant hum of sheer terror pulsing through Hope's veins—a terror that had begun over a decade and a half ago when her real life with Corbin started. The sweet scent of freshly cut grass drifted on the summer air, grounding her—for a heartbeat—in something that felt almost safe.

But even in that park, the shadow of her husband's words and omnipresent threats lurked in every cruel whisper of wind that brushed against her flesh. The rusty squeak of swing chains cut through the breeze, reminding her that she was never truly free.

When Fowley was full and content, Hope picked up what felt like her one-ton cell phone and called the number in her journal—the one from the pamphlet she'd found in her frenzied past two weeks during their move from San Diego, California, to Cambridge, Massachusetts.

"Hello?" a female voice answered.

"Um, is this a domestic violence shelter?" Hope stammered, words spilling from her lips. "I mean, I just saw this phone number on a pamphlet. I think I need help."

The woman on the other end reassured Hope that she had dialed the correct number, asked for a synopsis of what was happening, and then provided instructions for arranging a safe transfer and shelter for the night. When Hope arrived—with Jemma in one arm and Fowley asleep in the other—she was stunned to see that no one there had visible marks, broken bones, or missing limbs; they looked and sounded just like her or anyone else. As it came time for her to fill out the intake paperwork, Hope recounted her situation and admitted that she didn't think she truly belonged there. The intake specialist let out a light, but not unkind laugh. The petite woman with silver-rimmed glasses looked up, her smile as steady as the clipboard she balanced on ink-smudged fingers. The gentleness in her hazel eyes made Hope's shoulders sag in reluctant relief.

"Oh, honey, you of all people belong here. You just don't know that yet," the specialist said as she busily completed Hope's paperwork while another attendant cared for Fowley and Jemma played.

"Now, just so you understand, these are hard rules, and breaking any of them can lead to your expulsion." She outlined the non-negotiable rules, ending with a ban on any contact with Corbin. Hope's pulse hammered at the thought of silence.

"Tomorrow," she continued, "one of our advocates will accompany you to the courthouse to file for a Protective Order on behalf of yourself and your children. The advocate is there simply to support you but cannot help you complete the court paperwork—only your own words. And no phone calls to your perpetrator, do you understand?"

Hope's gut churned at the thought of being forced to go to court, so she asked if it was required. Yes, it was, or she would have no place or support there. Reluctantly, she surrendered, signed the papers, and after settling Jemma into her bed and Fowley into the diapers, pajamas and pack-and-play they provided, she opened the door to their room and looked out into the starry night sky.

Hope felt a nagging fear deep inside. "Is Corbin okay? Must he be worrying about us by now?" Her mind raced, pleading for the familiar terror to recede.

To quell her nagging feeling, she thought, "Oh, I'll just call him quickly to let him know that we're safe, and then I'll hang up after he knows we're okay."

Despite everything she had experienced in the last 48 hours, plus nearly 10 years, she clung to the delusion that her husband, in title only, still cared for or even loved her. Hope would later recall how hypnotic he was, possibly because he truly believed in the depths of his own deception, enabling him to convincingly and chillingly manipulate others with his untruths. With trembling fingers, Hope dialed his number.

When Corbin answered, his tone was harsh—not one of concern, but of command. Accustomed to fawning over and dismissing his cues after two decades of denial, Hope did not register the warning until it was too late.

"Corbin," her words came out soft and soothing. "We're okay. I just wanted you to know that we're safe, but I needed some time to think."

Corbin's response was sharp and quick. "I know where you are, Hope... A shelter? Really?"

Hope's throat tightened.

"You crossed the line," he growled. "Don't bother coming back." The phone trembled in Hope's numb hand.

"I would ask them about a Protective Order tomorrow morning, really. That's hilarious." Corbin laughed loudly and deeply, but then his voice leveled. "You might have 'your kids' for a while, but I will file something every day, every week, every month, and *twice* on Saturdays until those kids are mine! Then you'll never see them again."

Hope was suddenly left in deafening silence. Corbin hung up on her. The only sound she heard was the racing of her own caged heartbeats.

***

The next morning, bright and early, Hope roused her children to sign them into daycare, for the first time handing Jemma and Fowley off to utter strangers. Every step she took toward the courthouse felt like an act of rebellion against a fate she had been forced to endure. The thought of leaving her children in the hands of complete strangers twisted her stomach into knots—but staying in place was no longer an option.

As she approached the pillars and steps leading to the courthouse doorway, her heart dropped. This was Corbin's domain—power, money, control, and facade.

What if Corbin was right and the judge denied her Protective Order? Hope grasped the advocate's arm, trembling.

"I can't go in there! I—I just—this is his territory, not mine. What judge will believe me?" she whispered, her voice barely audible over the pounding of her heart.

"Listen," the advocate replied calmly but firmly, "I am not an attorney, and I have no legal training. I am here to support you. We'll move from here into the courthouse, and then we can go to the Clerk's Office where you will make your statement. I'll be right here with you. After you file, it's early enough in the day that a Temporary Hearing should be scheduled for the early afternoon. The judge will consider everything you write in your statement when seeking protection. Again, I'm not an attorney, and I can't tell you what to do or guide what you should say, but I can tell you I've walked beside many women through these doors and back out again. Are you ready now?"

Hope knew that after her phone call with Corbin, she had broken the rules— and there was no turning back. With trembling hands, she allowed herself to be led inside and through the process. She typed and deleted at least five drafts of her statement for the judge, her mind a torrent of fear and resolve, and finally filed her legal documents with the clerk, who set a hearing for 11 AM that same day. Time passed slowly as the advocate and Hope—battered but determined— waited on the middle row of benches in a hardwood-lined, darkened courtroom.

Hope's mind replayed every strangulation, every assault at knifepoint, every time he had shaken Jemma or hurt her in ways that made her cry, the assaults against her children who did not survive after birth, and the sound of his punches next to Fowley's tiny, screaming, flinching face echoed through the courtroom—each moment seared into her memory as sudden scars of forced, jolted, partial mental unraveling.

And then it hit her in the gut: all those broken household items, every shattered piece, belonged to Jemma. Her splintered toy hobby horse, her play table, her bedside lamp... these items belonged to the children, not to her. Their innocence was being systematically dismantled with every rageful outburst. With that revelation, Hope's fear heightened as she realized she had left not for herself, but to save her last living young children, Jemma and Fowley!

"All rise!" a voice called out. "The Honorable Mark Leyton Court is in session!"

The advocate led Hope to the plaintiff's chair. Left alone, this battered, broken wife and desperate mother had to explain, in her own trembling, fumbling words, why she needed the court's protection from her husband after a decade of mental battery that equaled his physical assaults, and why the court should protect Jemma and Fowley from their father.

What happened next blurred into a haze of formalities and fleeting moments of clarity. The judge granted the Temporary Protective Order, a slivered paper promise of thin protection that would soon be served upon

Corbin by the sheriff. From the moment the sheriff served those papers, Corbin would have the opportunity to appear in court and offer his mind-scrambling defense.

"He would win," Hope's mind raced at the thought of Corbin rewriting history about the things he had done to her over the years and to their children, as ice replaced any blood within her terrorized veins.

After filing the paperwork, Hope stepped onto the courthouse steps and, with shaking fingers, dialed her father. Jonesy—Joseph Uriah Livingston to the world, Dad to her—answered on the first ring and promised he'd be there before she could draw her next ragged breath.

She waited outside the shelter, checking once more on Jemma and Fowley, when Jonesy's battered pickup rolled to the curb, its Rhode Island plates dusted from the long highway sprint. He swung open the passenger door, his weathered face softening when he saw her. His carpenter's hands, calloused yet gentle—the same ones that built cribs, patched neighbors' roofs, and held communion cups—closed around hers.

Hope's voice cracked as she climbed in. "Dad, he believes his own lies. If Corbin can convince himself, what's to stop him from convincing a judge?"

Jonesy met her gaze, his eyes steady beneath the brim of his faded GO MILITARY cap from the branch he served in. "Then we'll make sure the truth is louder than his lies, honey. You're not alone in this."

The drive north toward Cambridge simmered under a muggy summer sky, each mile thick with the anticipation of confrontation. Jonesy sat solid and calm beside her, a wiry sentinel in a worn flannel, appearing almost fragile until one noticed the unflinching resolve in his eyes. Hope's pulse jittered, but her father's quiet, unwavering presence was the small, steady plank she could balance on while the storm raged around them.

***

Hope's heart hammered as she sat in her father's idling pickup truck, the Sheriff's cruiser looming a few yards away. Across the street stood the brick row house—a fortress that had doubled as her prison and, two nights earlier, had almost become her grave. Now that stronghold was about to be breached by the legal papers clenched in the Sheriff's fist.

In the still air, stirred only by Hope's unheard frantic heartbeat, her father's truck sat nearby, overshadowed by the looming Sheriff's car. Her powerful husband's stronghold was poised to be toppled by the legal documents clutched in the Sheriff's grasp.

"Are you prepared for this, honey?" her father's voice, calm yet edged with worry, broke through her reverie of crushing overwhelm.

Hope swallowed hard. "I have to be, Dad. I started this—I need to see it through," she said, her voice a mix of uneasy anticipation and shock.

Her father nodded, his grip firm as he took her arm. He removed his cap and ruffled his silver hair. Together, they approached the Sheriff's sedan, where the officer awaited them. Soon, they all moved toward the house's entrance, with the Sheriff urging Hope and her dad to delay until his job had begun, ensuring their safety with his presence as the sole legal enforcement. The door opened to reveal Corbin, his face contorted as he unveiled his grotesque mask for the first time to outsiders while the protective legal papers were presented and explained. The Sheriff's voice was cool and detached, declaring the terms.

Corbin's anger erupted like a volcanic surge. "That's what I get for marrying a G-D filthy whore!" he spat venomously. "Hope, everyone's going to know who you really are!"

Hope's father, Jonesy, responded swiftly and decisively. "We already know the truth about your wife, Corbin. Hope has laid everything bare before us all. She's got nothing to hide. You asked for her hand in marriage all those years ago? She knows about my letters and phone calls, too. You were my son, but no more, Mr. Dekker."

For a long moment, silence reigned. Then Corbin's fury subsided into a sinister calm as he attempted to mask his anger with a veneer of civility, extending his hand toward Jonesy.

Hope's dad did not flinch; his hand remained resolutely at his side—a silent moral rebuke. This refusal underscored the deep chasm of disdain between them, and Hope's father's presence was anything but fragile now.

Corbin's voice shifted as if he were rehearsing a new narrative.

"Mr. Livingston, my utmost intent has always been to cherish Hope and our family. Any harm was unintended; my life's dedication is to ensure her happiness."

Hope's husband's tone, though softened, was laced with manipulation that his father-in-law saw right through.

Hope's father tightened his grip on her arm. Having learned the hard way from his twenty-five years of marriage to Hope's cruelly remorseless and narcissistic mother, Hope could see it in her father's face—he had lived through this before. He had heard lies like these and survived the damage. He wasn't buying Corbin's act—not for a second.

"Going through courtroom scrutiny may dismantle all I've strived for, Mr. Livingston," Corbin continued, gesturing to the layer of legal papers with beguiling ease. "What good am I if stripped of my ability to provide financially and protect my own wife and children? If this—" he waved his hand dismissively at the Protective Order on his record, "robs me of the career and the educational opportunities that will provide for Hope and our children, sir, I won't be able to allow her to stay at home with them. Hope, isn't this what we've always wanted and worked for together?"

Hope's resolve trembled on the edge. Her father's presence steadied her—a beacon amid the dark storms of abuse. As Corbin's hazel eyes met Hope's father's, he was met only with a silent but heavy stare, causing Corbin to flinch as the tension thickened. Corbin's attempt to appear contrite was as skillful as it was hollow, and Jonesy, with his all-too-knowing and experienced ears, tightened his grip on his daughter's hand.

After the sheriff executed the order and ushered Corbin away, Hope's father locked all the doors and windows of the brick row house he knew his daughter would soon need to sell, doing so with deliberate care. He turned to Hope, who had held her composure in the face of her husband—her sixteen-year-long incarcerator, hostage-taker, and hijacker—but now, the dam of her forced restraint broke. She crumpled into her father's broad chest, tears streaming in torrents; a long-overdue outpouring of years of silent victimization, coercion, and inescapable suffering.

She tasted salt as tears slipped silently down her face, each one a quiet acknowledgment of the depth of her losses. It wasn't just the shattered remnants of countless houses that never became homes; it was pieces of her soul, years stolen away—the chance to know joy or discover who she might have been.

She felt the weight of all the broken things pressing down on her chest—the splintered table, the shattered baby pictures behind cracked glass, the ruined baby rocker. Each object told the story of a childhood robbed, a motherhood dismantled by someone who claimed profound, eternal love even while inflicting unbearable harm.

She heard the silence between herself and her father—vast, sacred, and heavy with all the years they'd lost to chaos. Yet within that quiet was something new: a fragile calm, a moment to mourn together, gather their strength, and perhaps finally begin the healing their family so desperately needed.

Author's Note

In this chapter, Hope must finally face glimmers of truths she has spent sixteen years forcing underground—truths about her own suffering and heartbreakingly, about what her children, Jemma and little Fowley, have endured. The judge's unexpected decision to grant a Temporary Protective Order should feel like deliverance, yet it flings her into unfamiliar territory: a domestic violence shelter and a courthouse that feel as foreign as another planet.

Tasked with writing her own statement for the hearing, Hope discovers that trauma has scattered her memories like shards of glass across a dark floor. Each time she attempts to gather these pieces of truth, Corbin's voice cuts through—*No one will believe you; this is your fault; fill in the blank, you cursed and twisted name.* Research supports her struggle: prolonged abuse can leave survivors feeling as though their reality is "irreparably fragmented" (National Domestic Violence Hotline, 2020).

As you enter Hope's raw, splintered memories, let her pain—so profound that she is "past feeling"—compel you to stand against the systems that allowed her voice, and her very sense of reality, to be slowly and methodically erased.

Chapter 8

Mother Erased:
Twenty Years through Seventeen Years Past, Bleeding Throughout Present Day

After this turbulent day, Hope returned to the domestic violence shelter—a place where finding even one bed was a miracle. Despite the turmoil and instability, she clung to the promise of safety that this temporary refuge offered.

In the days that followed, the shelter itself became another source of stress, turmoil, and confined desperation. They stayed in a small, cement-walled room with several cramped cots and battered mattresses. The air reeked of stale sweat and antiseptic, laced with the sour tang of unwashed clothes.

Three families, all strangers, were crammed into the tight space, each with their own clashing parenting styles. Privacy was nonexistent.

The walls bore scars of faded, peeling paint. A faint hum of murmured arguments and the cries of frustrated children never stopped.

In one corner, little Jemma, barely four, lashed out at another child with a sharp snap of her tiny hand, her voice raised in a bitter echo that made Hope's stomach twist. The words were too cruel for her daughter's age. Hope froze. The gesture—was that... Corbin?

A sick, familiar chill ran through her as she watched Jemma mimic movements she had hoped were buried in the past. Her daughter's little arm shot out again, her brows furrowed with a look Hope knew all too well. Had Jemma really seen and absorbed that?

Hope's voice caught in her throat as she rushed over. "Jemma, no, honey, we don't do that—"

But Jemma's face was already scrunched in confusion and frustration, her tiny fists clenched at her sides. Hope crouched beside her, unsure whether to comfort, correct, or cry. Her mind reeled. Was this just childish imitation— or had the violence already taken root?

Nearby, the faint cries of other children blurred into the air, but Hope could only hear the pounding in her chest. Fowley, still asleep beside her, stirred slightly in his bassinet, unbothered by the noise. How could her baby rest while the world remained this broken?

In the turmoil, Hope's mind raced with memories of better, safer times at her father's house, the only home she'd known—the inviting warmth of her childhood home, with its stone-built fireplace and quiet nights filled with gentle laughter with her father and friends when he had her.

It was during one of those sleepless nights, as Jemma whined about the bed and missed her pink bedroom in the old house they'd left in California, while Hope desperately ached to soothe Fowley's colicky cries, that a comforting, familiar presence cut through the overwhelming dread.

She clutched her knees to her chest, rocking slightly on the thin mattress, the cries around her fading into white noise. Just when the weight felt unbearable, her phone buzzed—jarring her back to the present. On the other end of the line was a soft yet insistent voice that heralded the arrival of her father. Her heart fluttered with a blend of hope and trepidation.

"Hope," a deep, gravelly voice nudged gently on the other end of the phone— revealing her protector and her father—Joseph Livingston, known to his closest friends as Jonsey. His once-military-hardened face now bore the lines of a carpenter's life, etched by years of hard work and silent post-divorce suffering.

"Come on over," he said in a measured tone that carried both command and compassion. "The home I built—where you spent half your childhood—is always open to you. It's away from all the noise, the mess of things. You knew where you were driving, Hope. Rhode Island was the right call. Bring the little ones, and let's be together again. There's room for you, Jemma, and little Fowley. It's warm—real warm—and safe, just like you remember. I've kept it cozy, mostly the same. I'm guessing the shelter isn't exactly home. I even picked up a little something for Fowley to sleep in. But you'd better hurry— the cornbread won't wait long," he added, knowing exactly how to tempt Jemma—and his daughter, too.

Exhausted but spirits lifted by her father's grace, Hope uttered the words, "Gramps *might* have cornbread," and 4-year-old Jemma raced to gather the few belongings she'd left Cambridge with and helped her mom collect their other things to officially exit the shelter. Hope blinked back a fresh wave of tears, clutching the phone like a lifeline. The thought of her father's warm kitchen, the soft lap of maple leaves in the Rhode Island breeze—it all felt surreal. Could she really go home again?

***

"My family," Jonesy's strong and reassuring voice called gently from the threshold of his home. His worn hands, calloused from years of labor, trembled only slightly as he offered a tentative smile. Beneath his full head of silver hair, his eyes were soft with empathy and determination. As he opened the front door and hoisted their sparse belongings into the mudroom, he wished to wash away the harsh memories of his daughter and grandchildren's time at the shelter, along with all the other experiences that had led his family back home.

"Come on in, kids," Hope's father said in a measured tone that carried both command and compassion. "This is the home I built years ago in Providence where your momma used to come back to when she was young. It is your home now, too—a safe place where we can all be together as a family. There's a room for you, this way, Jemma, and Hope, here's one for little Fowley, and here's your room, pumpkin." Jonesy showed his granddaughter her room while Hope's eyes brimmed with tears at seeing an actual crib for Fowley next to her own childhood bedroom. Her father had adjusted it to suit his daughter's new needs, with a plush rocker where she could tend to Fowley and ease the silenced pain that her father must have noticed somehow.

Inside her father's home, every detail spoke of stability and a promise of sanctuary. The entryway was modest but inviting, with hardwood floors that creaked softly underfoot and walls adorned with faded photographs of a bygone era. In the living room, his handcrafted stone fireplace dominated the space, its ancient, rugged surface polished by years of family gatherings. The glow of the fire danced across the room, creating shifting shadows that seemed to embrace all who gathered near it. The familiar scent of cinnamon apple cider and burning wood enveloped Hope, anchoring her memories to childhood safety and laughter.

Her dad led Hope into a sunlit room where his grandchildren played after Jemma devoured a slab of Gramps' cornbread, drizzled with raw honey while gulping her warm cider. Jemma's bright laughter echoed as she darted across the worn rug, her small hands reaching eagerly toward a paper airplane that her grandfather had patiently shown her how to fold from a simple sheet of paper. Fowley, wrapped in a soft blanket, gurgled and cooed contentedly as Hope handed him to her father. Jonesy cradled him with the careful tenderness of a man who had seen much loss and was determined to preserve every scrap of innocence in the aching ones surrounding him.

"Look at you two," Jonesy murmured, his voice low and steady as he gently ruffled Jemma's hair. "This is what family is all about. You're safe now, and we're gonna make sure nothing ever hurts you again."

Hope watched, tears glistening in her eyes, as her father's presence filled the room with a palpable sense of optimism and strength. It was a stark contrast to the harsh reality of the unsafe sixteen years with Corbin, followed by the past months spent at the shelter—a world where survival had meant sharing cramped quarters with strangers and echoes of past traumas. Here, at her dad's home—their home—the air was filled with the soft sound of her father's laughter and the crackle of the fire: a symphony of quiet resilience.

Later that evening, as Hope sat with him by the stone fireplace—its embers glowing like tiny beacons of defiance against the darkness of her recent past—they spoke in hushed tones about the future.

"Hope, you did good," her dad commended her, his voice warm yet tinged with sorrow. "You protected those kids, and you got yourself out, and that means everything to me."

"Thank you, Dad," Hope replied softly, her fingers trembling as they brushed against his calloused ones. "I just... I need to believe there's a way out of all this chaos."

Her father's eyes hardened with resolve as he added,

"We'll get through this, together, Hope. I built this house so that you and the kids could finally have a home that isn't a battleground. Forget the old address, forget the shelter—come live with me, where every brick and beam is meant to keep our family safe."

As Hope lay on her side in the bed her father had prepared for her, her mind drifted back to the day after the Protective Order was granted and served. Hope had been fortunate to find a place in the domestic violence shelter, but she soon found herself barraged with phone calls from her sister friends in California—mostly wives of the Bishopric and the Patriarch—offering scented word grenades, sending third-party messages of Corbin's "eternal love," "tormented regret," "dreadful sorrow for his actions," and "deepest desire to let Hope know that she was the most amazing wife, the best mother, and the beloved daughter of God that anyone could have asked for... if only he could somehow let her know..."

And so began more intentional brain thefts upon Hope.

This kind of third-party contact was sometimes included as an extension of Domestic Violence legislation and referred to as *Coercive Control* in other civilized nations outside the United States—prosecuted as felonious acts that are equally or more insidious extensions of Domestic Abuse and Interpersonal Violence (IPV).

In Hope's aftermath, those third-party people would have had her reconcile her "Temple Union to your High Priest," potentially leading to her and possibly her children's deaths. As she lay and slept on and off that first night in the bed her father had prepared for her, Hope's senses remained on guard and alert—a state known as hypervigilance, common in survivors of Complex Post-Traumatic Stress Disorder.

In the moments when her body relented to sheer exhaustion and slept, she would soon awaken in a cold sweat, unable to recall Corbin's now whitewashed violence but vividly remembering her husband's double life—something she had learned about by overhearing her Bishop's phone call the day after Corbin seemed to have meant to kill her by smothering her on the sofa. Hope shuddered at the revelation of Corbin's affairs with other men, at least equal to or greater in number than his strangulations upon her—at every house they had lived in, as though he had marked both her and his omnipotent reign against each surface, just before cutting off her airway to the edge of expiration.

The morning after Hope arrived at her father's home with Jemma and Fowley, the intrusive calls and messages bearing reconciliation attempts continued. The relentless pressure from her former Mormon community wove a tapestry of isolation around her. Every attempt to force her back into submission sent her down another spiral of confusion and betrayal by people she once considered trusted.

A cacophony of voices invaded Hope's every moment from the day after the order had been served—a relentless tide of emails, text messages, and phone calls, each one a calculated whisper meant to erode her resolve.

In her father's home, one call featured a stern, emotionless lawyer who intoned, "Hope, reconsider your stance. Reconciliation is not surrender; it is pragmatism for the children's sake." Another message, dripping with clinical detachment, stated, "Your compliance will ensure a smoother path forward. Our records indicate that a modified protective order is in your best interest."

The voices merged into a dissonant chorus that threatened to blur the horrific memories of sixteen years—of strangulations, of crippling assaults, and of secret, extramarital liaisons hidden beneath layers of deception.

***

Amid this assault—now on her own home turf—a new front emerged. New sister-friends from the Church of Jesus Christ of Latter-Day Saints began trickling by the Livingston home. Hope hadn't met these women before, not since the family's relocation from California. They came bearing casseroles and baked goods "for you and the kids," along with offers to rake leaves and help with the yard "during such troublesome times."

Their faces wore smiles too wide, too practiced. Their voices were soaked in saccharine tones, but their eyes flinched when they looked at Hope— when she didn't flinch back.

One of them tilted her head and asked, far too casually, "Really, Hope, how far will you take this? You have such a catch in Corbin. He's amazing!"

Hope said nothing. She didn't have to. Her refusal to lower the Protective Order spoke volumes—and it made them uneasy. Soon, their attention pivoted toward Hope's father, with rehearsed pleasantries aimed squarely at him.

"Mister Livingston," one sister began, nervously smoothing the hem of her cardigan, "our community's strength comes from unity."

Jonesy, seated calmly in his armchair, raised a single eyebrow. He didn't respond.

The second sister jumped in, her voice just a touch too bright. "We believe that embracing our faith—fully—will heal Hope."

She smiled, then added, "We've been linked through Divine Revelation from the Prophet Joseph Smith, and our Living Prophet today. There is more than the Old and New Testaments to the Plan of Salvation. Any means to return to our Heavenly Father must pass through the Atonement worked out for us by our older brother and Savior, Jesus the Christ."

Jonesy gave a small chuckle—not mocking, but amused.

"Hm," he said, leaning forward slightly, "that's interesting. If there's more than Biblical salvation through grace—and not through works—why didn't Jesus or His disciples ever teach it?"

The first sister straightened up. "Brother Joseph, the only man who communed with Jehovah directly, brought us these divine revelations. When the disciples were killed—as even our Prophet Joseph was martyred—the Priesthood was lost. It had to be restored so that full salvation could be revealed."

Jonesy's smile didn't waver, but his eyes sharpened.

"So," he said slowly, "what's this I've read about Joseph Smith having over thirty wives? Seems to me the Savior was pretty clear about one man and one woman."

Both sisters exchanged a glance, the second one answering cautiously. "That was a prophecy for a season only—necessary to fulfill the Lord's command. We now follow the current Prophet's direction."

Joseph pressed, his voice calm but unwavering. "And what about your current Prophet? Does he have more than one wife?"

The first sister blinked. "Oh no! That—polygamy—is no longer a practice, we assure you."

The father of this house leaned forward, clasping his hands. "I've read my Bible. I've also read the history books—you might want to visit both."

There was a pause. His voice grew firmer and lower.

"Joseph Smith inserted himself into your version of the Old Testament. But do you know what happened to prophets who made false prophecies in Scripture? They were stoned. That's not martyrdom. Smith, State

Governor of Illinois, was killed by a mob after he destroyed a printing press—trying to silence pamphlets that exposed his polygamous acts, including one involving his own stepdaughter. Some of those women were already married to his 'Brothers.' No children came from it—just secrets and control."

He let that land, then added, "If I had a brother like that, I wouldn't need an enemy. Wasn't your second Prophet, er President, Brigham Young, a State Politician too, and others after him?"

The sisters stiffened. One tried to speak, but Jonesy wasn't finished.

"And those 'Lord's curses' that Joseph Smith claimed would strike his killers? They never came. So was he a prophet... or a proph-EH-liar?"

His tone grew colder.

"If your current prophet were honest, he'd admit he's a polygamist too. After all, he remarried. So by your teachings, that's two wives waiting in the afterlife."

The sisters stared at him, lips parted, words caught behind their frozen smiles.

"You call yourselves 'The Church of Jesus Christ of Latter Day Saints,'" Jonesy said, "but that doesn't make you Christians any more than a piece of toast that states it is the New Christ."

He now stood, his voice unwavering. "Why would a true church need a hedge fund large enough to rank among the top four wealthiest in this country?"

With the weight of his faith behind every word, he delivered the final blow:

"You may want to consider your eternal consequences. In the Bible Christians read, it says—Deuteronomy 4:2: 'You shall not add to the word which I command you, nor take from it.' And in Revelation 22:18–19, the warning is clear: 'If any man shall add to these things, God shall add unto him the plagues.'"

"Your man, Joseph Smith, did you know that before he translated your additions to the Sacred Texts of the Bible, he was a charlatan? In fact, the Urim and Thummim he used were the same rods for which he charged people a wagonload of money to 'foretell' where water was when it wasn't."

"Please rest easy knowing we are fine. I will not be swayed by your empty promises or your sugar-coated, distorted, non-Christian lies. Leave my daughter, my grandchildren, and my home out of this by remembering to forget you ever knew this address or any of us who live here."

Hope observed her father closely, noticing the steady resolve in his voice. His words rang with conviction, making her heart swell with pride. Joseph's message resonated with the authority of his deep Biblical conviction. The stark contrast between his heartfelt, scripture-laden defense and their hollow, rebranded rhetoric was palpable—an unbridgeable chasm between the truth of his faith and the distorted doctrine they peddled.

***

Later, throughout these invasions, which continued and intensified through telephonic contact with Corbin and his foot soldiers, Corbin's intermediaries, in hushed tones over the phone, continued their orchestrated campaigns, urging Hope to "settle" on a divorce decree that would, in their words, "keep her safe and take care of the kids."

Their language was cold and bureaucratic, promising that a slight lowering of her protective order would "shield her" from the past—an unthinkable proposition that threatened to erase every memory of Corbin's brutal assaults and repeated betrayals.

Their calculated messages painted reconciliation as a virtue, a necessary compromise for the sake of practicality, even as they tried to reframe his history of abuse as a series of misunderstood "missteps."

Their coercion was relentless. Every call, every email, and every in-person visit by a third-party representative—be it a lawyer, counselor, or even a church elder—was a thread in the tapestry of control that Corbin wove around his wife and her children. Each word, each plea, was designed to fracture her memory, to dull the sharp edge of her pain until she could no longer remember the true horror of his sixteen-year reign of terror.

Their tactics were insidious, leaving her mind reeling and dissociated from the reality of her physical scars and emotional traumas.

"Hope."

Her father drew the line. "Your church people aren't right," he told her, his voice firm. "I can't have them here in this home and watch as you fade away while they drag you down. Please, honey—no more of their food, no more phone calls, or their forced well-wishes and visits."

Hope finally felt a pang of relief from her father's protection. Protection was a foreign concept in her later life until her return to his home. That night, together, Hope and her dad crafted a simple sign, its bold letters scrawled with both humor and warning:

"BEWARE Of DOG!"

It was a playful nod to Jonesy's loyal Great Dane, a gentle giant known to greet strangers with overwhelming affection rather than malice—a symbol of the unconditional protection and love he offered. The Church of Jesus Christ of Latter-day Saints, or the rebranded Mormon organization, had become no longer a pleasant welcome but a bitter reminder of the insidious crimes they hid to benefit Corbin and those like him while dismissing

Hope and her loved ones. The sign was more than a joke. It was the first line drawn—their boundary against spiritual manipulation, legal ambushes, and the coercion that had stolen so much. It warned not of danger from within the home, but of what waited outside, cloaked in kindness and carrying destruction. In that hand-painted warning, Hope saw defiance, safety, and her father's fierce love nailed into wood. To Hope, her father's home felt like a lifeline—a fragile sanctuary wrapped in cinnamon-scented warmth, where each creaking floorboard whispered of safety she barely dared to believe in.

Here, the vibrant strains of new music from Jonesy's Bible-based church filled the air with a promise of renewal. At her new church, Jemma danced with unbridled joy, her small feet pattering on the cool floor as she mimicked the Worship Leader's enthusiasm and sang, while Fowley began to wave his arms and bounce to the music; each child content in their classrooms, learning about the God who became flesh, who is and was the Word made flesh, unchanging in His inexplicable love, grace, mercy, and freedom from the Laws He alone could fulfill—a very different Jesus Christ than Jemma had been learning about in "The Church of Jesus Christ of Latter-day Saints," a Mormon organization filled with fear-mongering regimes and rules.

At home, with wide, curious eyes, Fowley quietly matured and attempted his first clumsy paper airplane under his Gramp's, Jonesy's, patient tutelage. As he learned to talk, one of his first phrases, after "Mama" and "Gramps," was "Pastor Mick," a playful reference to Lead Pastor Michael, or Mike, from the family's new church that had once been only Hope's father's family church. Gramps lovingly fixed up Hope's bicycle to be sturdier than before, so Jemma could ride it, which became a symbol of the freedom slowly returning to their lives; a fledgling freedom marked by gentle rides around the quiet streets lined with red maple and American beech trees, with Gramps patiently and protectively by his granddaughter's side.

For a time, the gentle cadence of life in Rhode Island offered a stark contrast to the turbulence of the shelter and the chaos and assaults in Corbin's world and Hope's mother's in Boston. Late at night, as Hope sat with her dad by the stone fireplace—its heat a tangible comfort against the chill of past abuses—they spoke of old memories: Hope's childhood visits, the soft murmur of growing optimism and resilience shared in whispered confidences. Jonesy's few, measured words held an unyielding promise of protection, even as he recalled with quiet anger the inhumane ways Corbin had injured his grandchildren during supervised visits and thrown years of handwritten letters to his daughter in the garbage to sever their relationship.

***

Even as new life blossomed in the warmth of her father's home, the shadow of Corbin loomed large in Hope's life. Through telephonic contact with third-party representatives alone, Corbin's voice, once manipulative and cold, now echoed with warm tones against her father's fireplace—words she had always longed to hear. His crafted messages urged her, both directly and through the third parties he deployed, to "collaborate" on a divorce decree that he insisted would "keep Hope safe and take care of her and the kids," even as he widened the metaphorical bloody hole in her mind and memory into a vast canyon of denial. His promises—delivered, not as threats, but as demands—made on the first night she entered the shelter when he instructed his attorneys to,

"File something every day, every week, every month, and TWICE on Sundays, until those kids are MINE! Then you'll never see 'your' kids again!"

quickly became lost in the recesses of Hope's mind, having been love bombed by Corbin through third-party contacts in the Church of Jesus Christ of Latter-day Saints and his peers in the military.

These waves upon waves of Corbin's third-party grenadiers left Hope reeling in a chasm of Corbin's creation, where she would vacillate between reconciliation or divorce followed by reconciliation through a **Covenant Marriage**—leaving her life at greater risk than ever, despite the physical safety her father now offered. There was no other protective provision in place to shield his daughter or grandchildren from the psychological warfare Corbin had declared upon his cherished daughter and his beloved grandchildren. Despite Jonsey's quiet objections, throughout hushed conversations with third-party Mormons, or members of the Church of Jesus Christ of Latter-Day Saint aka Mormons, and the private attorneys, who re-injured both Hope and her children, Hope was gradually persuaded to lower her protective order to allow for limited telephonic contact— ostensibly to "work out a Final Divorce Settlement" that would provide alimony for her lifetime medical needs and the welfare of her children while Corbin completed his program mandated by the Protective Order. Each flower-bombed voice, sweetened with promises of financial stability and reconciliation into a "Sacred Covenant Marriage," concealed ulterior motives, as Hope consumed the nectar and Corbin's bait. These actions by Corbin, facilitated through others, were extensions of "Domestic Violence," known as Coercive Control, which is classified as a felony in other civilized nations but not in the United States.

Despite the dissonance between the legal protections and the reality of Corbin's continued manipulations, his ultimate victory came when Hope was worn down into modifying the Protective Order to permit telephonic contact solely between herself and Corbin, as well as supervised visits with Jemma and Fowley, while he "saved money to pay for the treatments and protective and restorative provisions" he had agreed to in the Final Divorce Order.

These conversations between Hope and Corbin, along with visits involving Jemma and Corbin, served as constant reminders of the violence and neglect inflicted upon Jemma and Fowley. Hope pierced through the fortress of protection, shattering the haven that her father had worked tirelessly to create for his loved ones.

All the while, Corbin's legal team, armed with their resources and connections, manipulated every technicality to erode the walls that had once kept Hope's children safe. The legal system, tainted by systemic failures, became another weapon in Corbin's arsenal, gradually stripping away Hope's identity as a mother and diminishing every character trait that defined her, leaving her hollow and desperate at times, unsure of why she felt this way amidst what now appeared to be safe physical surroundings.

***

The divorce was agreed upon, signed, and entered by Hope's legal counsel before he withdrew from the case, just six months after Hope filed the Protective Order, which Corbin had successfully evaded.

The family felt a brief reprieve until Jonesy received a phone call, his hand trembling uncharacteristically as he handed it to his daughter and stood by her side.

"Hope Livingston, Attorney Robert Mandrake here, but you can call me Bob. Did you receive your Summons in the mail regarding my appointment to your case?"

"Summons? What is a Summons?" Hope replied. "I haven't gotten any mail. No, who are you?"

"It says sent to—wait, you live way out in California?" Bob's brisk voice questioned. "Are you located in California? I don't know if I can represent you if so." Attorney Mandrake sounded rushed.

"I haven't lived in California since my family moved about ten months ago with Corbin..." her voice trailed off. "What is this all about?"

"Ms. Livingston, as your In Forma Pauperis form indicates, I am contacting you as your court-appointed attorney regarding the hearing scheduled next Wednesday in Courtroom Number 5 concerning the Protective Order that you were temporarily granted, which Corbin Dekker, M.D., is now contesting. Before the hearing, while it isn't required, I like to meet my clients to thoroughly review their information and prepare the best case for those I represent."

"Now, when is the soonest you are available to meet? It will be at the law library nearby. Do you need directions?"

Hope was stunned, unable to gather her thoughts to form any words herself. Bob simply scheduled an appointment, provided her with driving directions, and then disconnected the call.

***

Hope was left in the kitchen, feeling lifeless; her father at her side as Jemma danced on the floor to "Million Little Miracles" and other Maverick City Music songs, the aroma of simmering chicken fajitas and homemade red enchilada sauce that Hope and her father were preparing together filling the air around them.

"Dad," Hope relayed, "Corbin is challenging the Protective Order...you know, the one served on him at the house in Boston before the divorce was finalized two weeks ago? Did we get some mail about it? I don't think... I can't drive myself there to meet the lawyer. Do you think Mrs. Gideon from church could watch Jemma and Fowley when we go meet him?"

Hope's dad nodded and moved to embrace his daughter. His weathered arms, filled with a father's love for the daughter who had brought a twinkle back to his eyes, encompassed her in a proper bear hug.

"I will make a call. You just relax. We will get through this together, as a family," her father said, his deep voice low and reassuring.

"I Won't Back Down" by Tom Petty suddenly played as Hope's father held her close, and they both felt somehow whole, knowing they were united as a family and would face life's storms together.

***

Sooner than desired came the day of the final protective order hearing, after the divorce had been finalized—a day that would test every ounce of her courage and spark a call to action against systemic injustice. The courtroom's hum was steady, like the ticking of a bomb in the background. The wood- paneled walls and imposing judge's bench pressed in on her as she rose, trembling, to testify.

"State your name for the record," the judge commanded, his tone neutral yet authoritative.

"Hope Dekker—er, Hope Livingston, now," she replied, swallowing hard.

"And you are here today requesting a hearing to commence on the current Protective Order against your ex-husband, Mr. Corbin Dekker?"

Hope nodded, "Yes, Your Honor," and her voice grew stronger.

Corbin's attorney, Ruby Victor, leaned forward with a predatory smirk, ready to pounce on any vulnerability.

The judge nodded. "Proceed."

Hope's attorney, Robert "Bob" Mandrake, then rose.

"Your Honor, we will demonstrate through both evidence and testimony that Mr. Corbin Dekker has engaged in actions that endanger Ms. Livingston and their children, Jemma and Fowley. These actions are not hypothetical— they have been observed and documented by professionals. Their divorce is finalized. The defendant has evaded this hearing for six months while harassing my clients without a single day's break in contact, using other people as go-betweens to further abuse all of my clients."

Bob presented affidavits from Jemma's physician and child counselors, describing not only the physical bruises on Jemma's hips and back following supervised visits but also the psychological trauma—nightmares, bed-wetting, and severe anxiety—that had overtaken her.

"Objection!" Ruby interjected.

"These affidavits are based on hearsay from someone I cannot cross-examine."

"Overruled," the judge replied curtly.

Bob then introduced forensic evidence from Mr. Dekker's personal computer.

"In Exhibit 3, Your Honor, these files were uncovered during a forensic investigation. The folder labeled 'My Daughter' contained inappropriate and illegal images involving minor females who appear to resemble one of the parties' minor children, the four-year-old girl. Coupled with Mr. Dekker's former counseling records—in Exhibit 8, which include discharge notes stating 'predatory behavior, sadism, diagnosed narcissism, sociopathic tendencies, lack of remorse. Lifetime intervention required until, if ever, there is a reintroduction to the parties' children,' as stated by experts here, Your Honor, the children are deemed at risk, as indicated in the conclusion section which states, 'unlikely to be safe around Jemma and Fowley unless the material expert that Corbin has signed and agreed to remain in treatment with agrees that his "rageful deviant, predatory behavior, clinically pre- diagnosed narcissism, and sociopathic behaviors" are each fully treated after a complete evaluation, followed by a customized intervention program director's approval that Mr. Dekker is cured of all of these listed here.'"

Bob didn't skip a breath as he continued, his voice steady and clear over the courtroom microphone.

"In Dr. Manhounen's expert report, Exhibit 9, it states that 'this reintroduction to the Parties' children is of utmost adverse concern, and unlikely to benefit these children, given the longevity and severity of Mr. Dekker's diagnosis and specifically his physical and other abuses upon them directly and upon their Mother in their presence.' This evidence raises serious concerns about Mr. Dekker's past and ongoing intent, capabilities, and mental state, particularly regarding the Parties' minor children."

Hope's breath caught as she recalled the horrifying moment the Forensic Detective called her with the news after she had given them the computer to examine. Her breath caught, her heart pounded in terror as the Attorney named the images that were said to resemble Jemma. What had Corbin done to her or to others like her?

Bob continued, "I now call a material witness: Mr. Joseph Livingston, the children's maternal grandfather."

After a brief objection, Mr. Livingston was sworn in. His testimony blurred into a charged dialogue with Judge Matthews as he described the pattern of Corbin's abuse.

He recounted specific incidents that Hope had forgotten from when Jonesy had visited them in California before their move—the broken baby rocker, Jemma's shattered table, and countless toys and personal items belonging to Jemma and Fowley that were violently thrown or smashed during Corbin's fits, some in front of him.

"I was present when Corbin beat his fist next to Fowley's head once, and when he took his belt...and used it on Jemma in ways no father or parent ought," Mr. Livingston testified. "He later told me—without remorse—'From one fellow Veteran to another,' he said that as a child he would break into houses with his older sister, rearranging the furniture and eating the occupants' food just to terrorize and confuse the homeowners."

"Corbin, my son-in-law, broke the Protective Order as soon as it was granted by calling me in an attempt to turn me against Hope. When confronted about the graphic images found on his computer, he downplayed them, backpedaling to claim he had never seen them and knew nothing of their content. He even twisted Hope's accusations, insisting that he had never done anything to cause Hope or Jemma to fear him. Well, Your Honor, Jemma lives in my home, and she says things and does things to her toys, to her new friends at my church, and even to her baby brother that are reminiscent of what her father, Corbin, would do or yell at her, at Hope, or her baby brother. Jemma's words and behavior corroborate all of my daughter's and my granddaughter's claims, as well as the sworn testimonies of the medical professionals that both Jemma and Hope see for care."

Corbin's attorney, Ruby, attempted to minimize these testimonies.

"Your Honor, my client acknowledges some incidents but denies their severity. The so-called injuries on Jemma were minor scrapes, and while the computer content is concerning, it does not directly implicate him as an immediate threat. Mr. Dekker is a decorated professional with no prior criminal record. Contacting the Plaintiff's father is not breaking the Protective Order in this state. He did not have direct contact with the Plaintiff until she lowered the Protective Order of her own accord to allow for telephonic contact between herself and my client, but not for his children. I would like to call my client, Mr. Corbin Dekker, to the stand."

After a long pause, the judge addressed Corbin:

"Mr. Dekker, you may speak."

Corbin adjusted his tie deliberately, his eyes narrowing slightly—a quiet but unmistakable sign of calculated control. "Your Honor, I love my children. Yes, I have made mistakes, but I have never intentionally hurt them or my ex- wife. I believe this proceeding is an attempt to alienate me from my children. Hope is trying to punish me for our divorce by using our children as pawns."

But Bob was not finished.

"Your Honor, may I cross-examine?"

After the Court agreed, Hope's Counsel questioned,

"Mr. Dekker, wasn't a favorite motto of yours in your Military Unit, 'Leave no witnesses, no trace behind?'"

Corbin remained cool as he quipped his response.

"No. No, that was not my motto. To clarify, one of my Unit's mottos was, 'Admit nothing, deny everything, make counter- accusations to confuse the enemy.'"

Bob ventured,

"Isn't that the same tactic you and your Counsel are using right now to confuse this Court?"

Ruby objected, and the Court sustained the objection. Bob didn't stop there.

"Mr. Dekker, to clarify, while you are an honorably discharged Veteran of the United States Military, you never served in any combat situations, did you?

Just to clarify for the record, in case Dr. Manhounen may have missed anything in his assessment, please state yes or no: did you or did you not serve your Nation in any wartime conflicts, either domestic or foreign?"

Hope noticed her husband's right temple vein twitch, and his strong, soft hands gripped the chair arms as he cut his reply short, simply responding,

"No."

Shuffling through papers, Bob continued,

"Typically, when a Veteran of your tenure and decoration departs from service, they are offered rights to lifetime benefits,

including medical care for themselves, but also for their spouses, I believe."

Bob probed,

"It looks like you departed from service but refused and severed any provisions like this and all others typically afforded to honorably discharged veterans."

Bob's eyes locked with Corbin's as he continued.

"Did you refuse those benefits and sever your rights to any of those provisions to avoid a trial like this in a Military trial, Mr. or Admiral Dekker?"

At that, Corbin nearly flew out of his chair in defiance, hollering,

"I NEVER answered to any Military trial! My Unit makes our own laws, and we keep them! I report ONLY to the United States President, and so does my Unit and my Team!"

Hope's knuckles turned white as she felt Corbin's cold, calculating gaze fixed on her.

The judge raised his hand to silence both Corbin and Ruby in advance.

"Mr. Dekker, you may step down, provided that Counsel is finished. Please let my Bailiff help you back to your seat if needed."

Corbin grew pale, and to Hope's fright and validation, as if a light switch had been turned on, Corbin's entire demeanor changed as he adjusted the suit Hope had purchased for him while stepping down and returning to his chair.

The Judge's voice seemed to echo through the courtroom. "Ms. Livingston, do you wish to make a statement?"

Hope stood, her legs trembling yet her voice resolute but strained.

"Your Honor, I lived with Corbin for sixteen years. We were married twice; the first was a Catholic wedding, and the second was something called a 'Sealing' for Eternity in the 'Church of Jesus Christ of Latter-Day Saints,' or Mormon Temple, not a typical church ceremony. Corbin never left external marks on me, but that does not mean I wasn't hurt. The injuries are internal, and the fear is constant. I did not sleep because I was always waiting for the next outburst aimed at me or our children. Corbin has physically hurt each of them from birth until now. Jemma, she's just four, and Fowley was only an infant when I fled for their safety—perhaps even more than for my own."

"When he, um, Mr. Dekker, Corbin, threw and broke things, they were not random objects—but our children's cherished belongings. This isn't just about the children, but I ache just breathing. I can't tell if it's damage to my spine, neck, and tailbone from being thrown across rooms, or from being strangled nearly to death too many times, or the last time when Corbin smothered me with pillows. He used to say often that there are worse things than dying, and Your Honor, his actions and how I feel after these years with him help me begin to understand his promises each moment. This is not hypothetical—it is my life and our children's. And if you do not protect us today, Corbin will use every resource he has to destroy us, just as he has promised."

The courtroom fell deathly silent.

Hope bit her tongue to stifle her overwhelming fear and trepidation as the judge thoughtfully tapped his pen, deep in thought about his looming decision.

"This court is responsible for protecting those who cannot protect themselves. Based on the evidence presented and testimonies given, I am granting the Protective Order, as there is a preponderance of evidence that domestic violence has occurred, specifically regarding life endangerment concerning the Parties' minor children. Mr. Dekker, you are hereby prohibited from any further contact with Ms. Livingston and the children, Jemma and Fowley Dekker—whether in person, by phone, or electronically. The Livingstons will leave first, and the bailiff will ensure you exit the courtroom no sooner than fifteen minutes after they depart. Is that clear?"

Hope's breath caught for a moment, stuck between a sob and a gasp. For the first time in her lifetime since Corbin, this courtroom didn't swallow her truth. She clutched the table for balance, tears slipping down her cheeks unchecked.

Corbin's jaw clenched, his nostrils flared. He stared straight at Hope, unblinking—daring her to feel safe. Ruby whispered sharply to him as his eyes burned with a promise of retribution.

***

As Hope left with her father, the courtroom behind them, her heart pounded with a fleeting sense of victory—a defiant call to action against a broken system. Bob rushed to catch up with them.

"Hope," Attorney Robert Mandrake beckoned as he gasped for air and jogged. Hope and her dad stopped short, and Bob soon caught up. Hope began to rush on in thankfulness and relief, tempered by awe that Bob had taken on this case, wading through only pieces of their looming legal filings.

When Bob met the two, his next words were ones Hope carried with her for the rest of her life:

"Ms. Livingston, I will be direct. This was a significant win for you today, especially for your children. It is uncommon for children to be included in a Protective Order, much less to have an Order for them alone, with no mention of challenging you, his former wife. I must ask you, why did you go through a divorce already?"

Their counsel's question landed flatly before both Hope and her father; their minds struggled to grasp the question.

Hope felt a prickle of anxiety as she heard her father's vague reply.

"They were married. Hope had to leave; she had no choice. When you're married and then leave, you get a divorce. Corbin told us..."

Bob interrupted Jonesy.

"Respectfully, Mr. Livingston, under normal circumstances, this would make sense."

Their court-appointed attorney, Bob, continued,

"If I were in your situation, I would have taken them and run— overseas— anywhere but stayed close to home; and no divorce. Now, you're all stuck,"

he added.

Hope was stunned as the words escaped her, just above a whisper.

"He would have found us. All of us. There's no place to run. Not for us."

Slowly, their legal counsel turned his head and locked eyes with Hope, whispering back with a shuddering knowingness.

"You are probably right."

Bob's mind wandered to the many missing children ads in stores and the alerts he received alongside every other cell phone owner, knowing that most of these missing children were caught in the crossfire of one of the millions of high-conflict divorces in their area each year. It troubled him not knowing whether the children behind the pictures and headlines were in the hands of a protective or perpetrating parent, or a caregiver who wanted them for their own agenda, or in a desperate attempt to create safety for unsafe children. **This case was different. The facts were all there. Never had he given any client this advice.** A chill ran down the back of his neck, but he disguised his shudder and shrugged it off, rolling his shoulders back into a confident stance.

Bob shook his tearful and grateful clients' hands, and they parted ways. That night, he had whiskey and held his family extra close. He had invested in Doberman Pinschers and his shotguns for a reason. He explained what little he could to his wife after their children were asleep.

Corbin Dekker was one of those people no one could run from.

***

Hope embraced her father tightly, lightly teasing him about his "big win" to cover herself and her dad from the growing, nagging sense deep down within her. She knew that Corbin was far from finished with his war against her, but brushed her feelings aside, as she was so accustomed to doing to accommodate the influence of others.

That evening, as Hope sat at her father's kitchen table with a warm cup of tea, her father, Jonesy, spoke with a mix of pride and sorrow.

"You did good today, Hope. You protected those children."

"So did you, Gramps," she replied softly. "I wish I'd known you'd take the stand."

"Surprise witness," Jonesy smiled gently. "I told Bob that your statement needed a little extra weight."

Hope could only stare at him—this man who had carried her brokenness like sacred cargo. She wanted to freeze time, to memorize the warmth in his eyes, to wrap herself in the silent courage that radiated from every weathered line on his face.

"He won't stop, Dad," she said slowly. "I know him better than anyone. He'll find a way."

"But Hope, you're divorced. The judge saw all the evidence. Jemma and Fowley, they are both safe, honey, along with you. You're free. We're a family, and we can finally heal now, together."

Hope's father's lined face, wearied from the day, looked relieved as he spoke. After Hope washed the dishes, they all sat by the fireplace, as Gramps rocked his grandson to sleep, and Hope played with Jemma on the plaid woolen sofa. "Reckless Love" by Cory Asbury and other songs streamed through the retired carpenter's living area and adjacent rooms, as if sensing the family's need for divine love, protection, and healing.

Three days and two nights passed.

Hope could feel it in the back of her mind—Corbin was planning something. The silence wasn't peace; it was a strategy.

Jemma began acting like Corbin had before they'd left, Gramps catching her just as she slammed the wall next to Fowley, who cried in the crib that a friend from his church had given them before their first night's welcome to his home.

"He's up to something, Hope," her dad sensed. "Expecting it too, are you?"

Hope nodded as she held Jemma in a time-out while Gramps walked Fowley across the wooden floorboards near the rustic woolen sofa; pillows sparse, the comfort in the fine craftsmanship of the piece alone.

Suddenly, five days after the Protective Order hearing, Hope's phone rang relentlessly with legal notifications. Within sixty days of the Protective Order, after the protective divorce decree was signed, the motions came like machine-gun fire—fifteen in sixty days. The shortest one? Nearly sixty pages. Her head spun with legalese she could barely make sense of—each page another assault, another attempt to rewrite the past and to assassinate her character as a mother, wife, and human, falsely accusing her of things her assailant had done himself.

Corbin's malevolent promises were coming true. In the aftermath of the Protective Order hearing, Hope clung to the solace provided by her father, Jonesy—a steadfast pillar amid chaos. His work-worn, calloused hands and unwavering heart full of steadfast love for his daughter and grandchildren kept Hope anchored. His resilience and hard-earned wisdom gave her the courage to face each new day.

"I'll file something every day, every week, every month, and twice on Saturdays until those kids are mine!"

Corbin's words twisted through Hope's mind like a cold, coiled serpent, leaving her as fragile as a raft lost in a stormy sea of legal madness orchestrated by Corbin and his well-paid attorneys before the divorce. Likely, the morning after Hope landed in that shelter, immediately after his promise, those words would forever echo through Hope's mind and wrench her gut just as when she'd learned about the images on Corbin's computer.

***

As the days swiftly passed, the legal onslaught continued, with more court hearings scheduled and without the help of a court-appointed attorney. Hope's father remained steadfast at his daughter's side as her shield and rock. All the money she had made from selling the house in Boston was quickly consumed by retaining the only attorney willing to take her case. Corbin, wielding the full force of his power, prestige, wealth, and connections, unleashed a series of legal motions that were at least as extensive as his initial filing, which spanned over sixty pages. Each document was a laser-guided explosive—a weapon in the form of meticulous filings intended to confuse the new judge, dismantle the existing finalized divorce decree, and ultimately fulfill Corbin's promises to strategically countermand and annihilate Hope's essence, her character, and obliterate every facet of her identity and her rights as a mother, ultimately separating her from her loved ones.

Courtroom after courtroom bled into the next, each one a box of harsh lighting and cold stares, where Corbin's legal team stacked motions like bricks meant to wall her off from her own children. The language of the legal filings was clinical and cold, using terms that bore only resemblance to Corbin: "emotionally unstable," "vengeful," "manipulative," "violent," and "unfit," as if measuring Hope's character could be quantified in legal jargon descriptive of Corbin.

In the sterile confines of the courtroom, Hope's testimony—a raw, painful recounting of the terror and abuse she had endured over a decade—felt like an assault on her very soul. Each word, each tear that fell as she recounted the bruises hidden beneath her skin, was met with dismissive glances and the steady, relentless tapping of a judge's gavel. In those moments, the protective order, which had once given her a glimmer of victory, turned into a symbol of her isolation and hopelessness.

The legal abuse was not just in the documents but in every whispered conversation outside the courtroom, in every call from the new attorney who assured her that her sacrifices would win out in the end. The court suddenly became a system that rewarded the abuser—a labyrinth of laws that erased the truth and her own memories, the very fabric of her world swapped out by a narrative in which Corbin was not only justified but victorious.

Hope's new attorney tried to keep up with the blitzkrieg of legal tactics initiated by Hope's ex-husband, but had other clients as well and simply could not manage every single lengthy motion without unlimited payments from Hope. She knew that the Church was paying for Corbin's townhouse rental, his food, and other personal bills, giving him every last penny of his high six-figure income to spend on a league of lawyers. Hope now had no income and no way to earn any, given the impact of Corbin's physical injuries on her. She rose above her psychological injuries to be present for

Jemma, Fowley, and her father. They each needed her; she vowed not to allow Corbin the satisfaction of breaking her abilities as both mother and daughter, despite his unmasked attempts to annihilate her capacity to parent Jemma and Fowley with her father's help.

***

Soon another court date was set. The courtroom's stale air unfurled before Hope and her father in an overpowering atmosphere of uncertainty, their family's lives in the balance. The overhead lights buzzed faintly. A bead of sweat slid down her spine. Her tongue stuck to the roof of her mouth like glue. The court's wood-paneled walls, the imposing judge's bench, and the relentless ticking of someone's wristwatch seemed to measure her physical pain.

When her case number was finally called, Hope rose with trembling limbs to face the judge. Her testimony unfolded in harrowing fits—a chronicle of abuse and terror, where past violations collided with present fears until truth and despair merged indistinguishably.

Corbin's attorney insisted that, as a material witness, Hope's father remain in the courtroom while she cross-examined his daughter for over an hour, and this new judge agreed.

When the Livingston's attorney called Corbin Dekker to the stand to go through the transcript of the protective order hearing, Hope felt lost.

As Corbin began to openly acknowledge and detail the various ways he had physically and otherwise harmed his wife—minimized and dismissed but accurately described onslaughts of strangulations, assaults, and other incidents—he flatly denied any wrongdoing against Jemma or Fowley. Simultaneously, he attacked their grandfather's account and character witness, staring at Hope's father as he spoke. Hope noticed her father's hand tremble in hers. She followed his vacant gaze and saw nothing but fog in his eyes. *Had Corbin's courtroom antics drained him too?*

That afternoon, after the brief hearing ended, Hope walked beside her father toward the parking garage. The air felt thick—too still, too quiet— like the world was holding its breath. As they reached the stairwell, she felt his hand falter against hers.

"Dad?" she asked, turning just in time to see him stagger, his face suddenly pale, eyes clouded.

Panic shot through her chest. She grabbed his arm, trying to steady him, but he leaned hard against the wall, taking shallow breaths, his lips slightly parted as if trying to speak.

The realization hit her like a punch: this last courtroom round had broken him.

He had sat through every word—heard the man he'd trusted with his only daughter openly admit to acts that were beyond multiple felonies against an animal, much less a person. Hope's father had relived every moment she had tried to shield him from. He'd been forced to watch her bleed out truths he never wanted to know, powerless to stop it, to protect her, to preserve her as he had promised in his heart. And then Corbin had twisted it all—attacked his name, his love, his legacy as a father and grandfather, and his daughter. She saw it now—the weight of it pressing against him from all sides.

"Dad, please, stay with me," she whispered, but even as she said it, a horrible understanding settled into the sinews of her bones and the marrow within them. Her father collapsed on the concrete of the parking garage adjacent to the courthouse.

Hope screamed. Their phones were not allowed in the courtroom for non-lawyers and non-court personnel, and she could not call for help. Their cell phones were still locked in his scarred pickup truck.

As the long scream caught in her throat, she remembered to yell "FIRE!!!" when no one would come otherwise to help.

The parking attendant soon ran over and dialed for an ambulance.

***

At the hospital, doctors confirmed that Hope's father, her children's Gramps, and only to those close to him, Jonesy, had suffered a massive stroke. Hope sat by his bedside, as much as the staff would allow, holding his hand and whispering words of a daughter's love and gratitude. She held his fingers like she used to wrap around his thumb as a child. The monitors beeped, mocking her helplessness. She wanted to scream but didn't want him to hear fear in her voice—not now.

In his final moments, Joseph Uriah Livingston squeezed his daughter's hand gently before passing away, his glimmering, tearful eyes glossing over as his eyelids were forced closed.

Hope could not hold back the tears of grief, pain, and anger. She didn't eat. Couldn't sleep. Every breath felt like betrayal—like inhaling without him was proof that she'd moved on. She hadn't.

Why did that judge have the sole right to insist on her father being in that courtroom; to force him to sit still and silenced to hear the inhumane and gruesome acts that Corbin freely admitted to committing against his treasured daughter when, as a dad, he was stifled and forced through explicit details, knowing that he would never have been able to protect her? To further sit there idle as Corbin switched things up and lied about what he'd done to Jemma and Fowley; to discredit her dad's truthful and last breaths to protect his family? How were any of these court or judicial decisions right or legal?

"Who was the court supposed to be protecting?" Hope thought as she sobbed.

"It sure wasn't my dad. He didn't deserve this—none of it, and neither do our children."

***

Jonesy's loss devastated his daughter.

Despite her grief, the legal battles raged on, as did motherhood.

Corbin's haunting promises echoed relentlessly as he made them come true:

"I will file something every day, every week, and TWICL on Saturdays, until those kids are MINL! And you'll never see YOUR kids again!"

Corbin's testimony in the Protective Order crashed through her mind as one of his hands shoved her head into the wall.

"I would like to clarify what my motto is, however; admit nothing, deny everything, make counter-accusations."

Hope had long since passed the point of feeling when, in court, Corbin's lawyer called Jemma's counselor to the stand to review session notes from fifteen months prior.

"Ms. Layton, in your notes here, you have written that Jemma said, 'I miss my Mommy. This is your handwriting, isn't it?'" Jemma's counselor nodded, confirming it was her handwriting and that it was indeed Jemma's statement.

"Weren't you confused when you wrote this, Ms. Layton? Could Jemma have missed her mother? She was there with her. See? In your notes, it states that 'Mom is in the room, detached, disengaged, etc.' My word, Ms. Layton! Jemma has been with ONLY her mother since this whole debacle of a fake Protective Order began, and hasn't seen her FATHER in over a year now. Didn't you intend to write, 'Jemma misses her DAD'?"

"Corbin picked an attorney who operated with the same motto," the thought crossed Hope's mind, but in court, stifled by the rules of procedure, she was left unable to voice what really happened.

Only her attorney could speak for her.

She scrawled on the yellow legal pad between them.

"Jemma DID say she missed ME! WHY? For these fifteen long months, she's LOST ME! I have been bombarded by Corbin's third- party interlopers trying to get me to reconcile our window-dressing marriage, scrambling through this attack of baseless hearings, more counseling sessions, school, life—but WE don't get time to OURSELVES!"

Nonetheless, when the judge asked, Hope's new legal representative stood, cleared his throat, and stated,

"No cross-examination, Your Honor," leaving Hope voiceless once again.

Hope's body went limp in the chair. She felt life simply leaving her behind.

***

Through relentless legal maneuvering and grueling court sessions in which Corbin's attorney unleashed barrages of unfounded accusations, Corbin managed to overturn previous rulings from a full Evidentiary Protective Order issued solely for their children and the entire protective divorce decree that he'd written with Hope and signed, ultimately securing full legal and physical custody of Jemma and Fowley, now casualties of Corbin's crosshairs, punished for daring to leave his near-lethal abuses.

Just one and a half years earlier, these two young children had been fully protected after an Evidentiary Hearing on their very own Protective Order. Now they were in the hands of those who had repeatedly harmed them and inflicted terror in their minds. This new judge ruled in favor of Corbin, fully dismissing expert evaluations and the need for Corbin's treatment plan and lifetime intervention, which he had previously agreed to and that their former Bishop had funded. Corbin had placed his name and documents in the divorce decree that was already signed and entered. But now, this new judge suddenly deemed all these protective measures to be "expensive and an unnecessary burden for their father to bear," and therefore, no safety measures for Jemma and Fowley were enforced by the court; the new judge wielded his power with the unchecked authority of **"Judicial Discretion."**

The final, crushing blow came when Judge Bullock issued a gag order against Hope, forbidding her from speaking about her marriage to Corbin, the abuse she had endured under his rule, or the ongoing proceedings that led to the effective kidnapping of her children by their perpetrator, with the threat of incarceration for any violation. This silencing was a profound psychological wound that deepened Hope's trauma and isolated her when she needed to talk, mourn, process, and be heard the most.

She had no rights. Not as a mother, not as a patient. Everything in that divorce decree—Corbin's signature, the promises, the protections—was just erased. How was that even legal? How could she not have known what else she could have done? Too late, they said. Always too late. She wasn't even aware that she had the right to sue Corbin in civil court for the lifetime disabilities her body bore, and that, as a result of Corbin's legally allowed delay tactics involving their children, all statutes of limitations had now far expired when she finally asked about her own care—after Corbin stripped away his responsibility for the agreed-upon medical care she needed due to his actions.

As she grappled with the courtroom's final decree, wandering outside the courtroom and through the now-memorized labyrinth of corridors and elevators, Hope faced a chilling truth: How would she stitch together the remnants of her shattered identity now that Jemma and Fowley were beyond the realm of her protection? What awaited them under Corbin's manipulative hands, subjected to mental gymnastics as mere children with no protector to shield them, while she remained their last line of safety? Could she ever regain her identity as a mother, a bastion of protection for them? What of her identity as a woman who once dared to dream beyond the boundaries now cruelly enforced upon her? How would she explain to Jemma that she needed to go with the man who hurt her and those she loved? Hope and Gramps had promised to keep her safe from Corbin, and that his overt promises that "kidnapping is okay" would be fruitless. How could Jemma ever trust her again? Fowley had never met him as a coherent toddler; what would happen to them now, with no one to intercede or chronicle Corbin's torrents of psychological and physical wrath upon them, as Hope's children and extensions of her life, in Corbin's cruel mind?

Within these shattered reflections lay the soul of a mother—erased by unyielding cruelty. Hope's truth remained close: every stolen moment fueled the fire of justice.

With her father dead, her children violently ripped from her protective arms, and her voice stifled by the law, Hope stood at the brink of despair.

Everyone she held dear had now been stripped away, leaving her empty, raw, and bloody inside. The stench of raw and rancid meat occupied the space where her heart once was.

***

Outside the courthouse, clutching the final custody order in her trembling hands, she read the words over and over, unable to comprehend the injustice. The letters bled into one another. Jemma's name—Fowley's name—were both there, stamped and sealed. Gone. Her children's names looked foreign on that page—as if they belonged to someone else now. Was this how motherhood ended? With ink and a judge's cold indifference? Her knees gave out before the scream could reach her lips.

"How could this happen?" she cried in irreparable anguish.

"How could a man convicted of domestic violence and child endangerment gain full custody except through a system that condones, dismisses, permits domestic violence, and protects the perpetrator instead of the victims?"

Stunned and shell-shocked, the question loomed in the air—unanswered, deafening—a rallying cry for change that Hope could not muster.

Then a final thought struck her: "If the Seventh Amendment guarantees a trial by jury for matters over twenty dollars, weren't her children's lives worth infinitely more? And what of her father's sacrifice? Of her battered soul, mind, and body?"

Hope sank onto the steps at the side of the courthouse as a car sped past, blaring Depeche Mode's song "Where's the Revolution." Hope wept without restraint. The shattered frame that once held her children's baby pictures suddenly became her world; she now replaced the frame that had once held the memories behind the shattered shards of glass.

Her body shook, her voice silent—a mother erased by the very systems that were supposed to protect her. And still, no one saw. No one asked. No one knew the world had just lost a father, a grandfather, a caring and protective mother, a family, and perhaps the last spark of hope.

Her anguished, muffled sobs represented missed opportunities—one for every passerby, every mother, father, grandparent, Court Servant, State Trooper, local police officer, honorable Active Duty Military member, Veteran, and anyone with a spark of human kindness who could rise, challenge the broken systems, and demand justice for victims like her.

As this broken mother and daughter wept outside the courthouse, no one stopped to ask what was wrong. Each person was too absorbed to see, to hear, to ask, or to answer.

***

Author's Note

This story is not fiction. It reflects the legal and emotional torment endured by domestic violence survivors every moment throughout the United States when the very systems that claim to protect them become weapons of further harm. Hope's journey, along with that of her children and her father, is truth; of navigating not just the trauma of abuses, but also the brutal gauntlet of **abusive litigation, coercive control, War Crimes perpetrated by U.S. Military upon citizens and Spouses as Domestic Terrorism, and false claims of parental alienation vs. natural child estrangement made by the perpetrator against the protective parent in the relationship.**

According to the National Crime Victim Law Institute, abusive litigation is the misuse of legal processes to harass, intimidate, and exhaust victims. It is a form of continued abuse, cloaked in legal legitimacy, used by perpetrators to control, punish, and break their victims long after physical separation. And it's happening in courtrooms like yours, all across this nation; to further abuse both adult and child victims alike; even those with a proven legal history of abuse; like Hope and the children she nurtured and would have given her life to protect. Their grandfather did.

Hope's family's battle reveals a broken legal landscape where constitutional rights protect the accused far more than they shield the innocent. The courts become arenas of re-traumatization. Protective legislation exists in name only unless it includes laws that safeguard victims from weaponized legal proceedings. To this author's knowledge, one state has taken a stand; others have not. The question isn't *if* it can be done; it's *why hasn't it been done where you live?* **The state that has these protective provisions, enacted them during the height of a global shutdown, or the COVID-19 outbreak pandemic.**

If then and there, why not **where you** *live? Why* **not as a nation,** *and why not now?* As you read, pay close attention to the signs—Corbin's manipulation, the misuse of parental alienation claims, the weaponized custody battles, and the emotional and spiritual toll it takes on Hope's family. Or will you too choose to look away from Hope? After experiencing this one of too many true similar stories, are you more of an accomplice to Corbin or a help to those like Hope and her children?

In this one of billions of similar stories; you must choose a side.

Who do you find yourself aligning with—Corbin Dekker and "his kids" or Hope Livingston and her family?

Ask yourself: **If Hope were your child, your sister, your friend—what protections would you demand for her and for these two young, innocent children?** Then act. Make notes. Start conversations. Share this book. Purchase the companion books—*Hope's Legacy* and *Identity Heist: Advocacy*—for ways to help move Hope's legacy forward, including healing and legislative reform ideas from her research and mine as her journalor. Contact your legislators. Demand national and local reform or her children and for the voiceless women like her and her loved ones. Use this story as a catalyst to make systemic changes *before it's too late* for another family like Hope's. Because silence, indifference, and inaction are accomplices to injustice—and to real-life perpetrators like Corbin.

What side are you on, without a middle ground?

Chapter 9

For Time and All Eternity: 18 through 21 Years Past

Following Hope's losses, she returned to her father's home in Rhode Island. His hand-built creation was the only sanctuary she had labeled as a home. With the recent, sudden, and unnecessary death of her father—who had been protecting her and his grandchildren after a mutual divorce was signed, finalized, and entered with the court—this place became her last refuge. In the midst of a cruel twist of what is labeled "justice" in today's family courts, which are as tainted as the crimson red of Hope's internal bloodstains from the turbulent years in Corbin's arms— her husband and her children's legally established perpetrator of assault— who had used the legal system to kidnap the two young children he had been found to have harmed, her father's home now felt as though it ached and bled along with her.

In the sanctuary of her father's home, a bequeathed gift, Hope took time for deep introspection as she tried to remove the traces of Jemma and

Fowley's lives from their grandfather's house, unable to erase the memories that were now hers to bear in solitude.

Some days, her sobs seemed endless, tears flowing from her reddened, splotched face as she rocked back and forth on the bare floorboards, her cries unheard by the outside world. A shattered mother moved with the only comforting motion she had given her babies, now offering her an unspeakable outlet; her simple rocking motion somehow soothed her as she ached from the indescribable losses of the children she would have died to protect—torn suddenly and physically ripped from her arms amid their own tears and shrieks. Those silenced cries for help remained forever captive within Hope's memory alone.

While Hope was reeling from these unthinkable losses, she had no idea that she had an opportunity to appeal the judge's hideous actions and incredulous final ruling, but only for a small window of time, which ultimately lapsed. The statute of limitations was far too short for her or any domestic violence victim still being victimized through the family court or through her children by their perpetrator to recognize, especially without the money to afford expertly trained legal counsel to represent their interests or those of their children.

It felt as if fate or God were rubbing alcohol and salt into the festering wound of her raw and rancid heart as time passed. Hope's only option was to appeal to the family court judicial board of Judge Bullock's peers and to make a judicial appeal.

Hope's glimmer of trust in any protection for her abused and endangered children was hurled against the towering red granite cliffs of Rhode Island's coastline and shattered by the Judiciary Board's stony response. Her hands trembled as she read and reread the words on their governmental letterhead, detailing their sole, unchallengeable, judiciary-bound final determination.

"...Judge Bullock was and remains within his right, and we, the entirety of his peers, based on his use of his own *Judicial Discretion* in these and all matters before him..."

As Hope limped through her father's home, the fresh scent of pines from the open windows overwhelmed her. She was aghast that these judges wielded God-like power, which she had been taught was supposed to ensure that every governmental body had another to check and balance; yet this one clearly had no one to answer to and bore no consequences for the wreckage left in the aftermath of their gavel rulings.

Perched on one hip, then the other, on the beautifully cushioned rocker her dad had given her to rock her children in, her mind was void of how she had come to be unable to sit on her tailbone, so deformed from the breaks under Corbin's rule and the numerous other injuries she had managed to hold together for the sake of her children and her father, with decades of adrenaline overload that crashed when her loved ones were gone.

This forced forgetfulness stemmed not only from the psychological impact of minimizing, whitewashing, and dismissing Corbin's physical assaults upon her by her Mormon, then Latter-Day Saint, priesthood leaders and other third parties, but was worsened by the illegal gag order imposed on Hope by Family Court Judge Bullock's ruling. If Hope had allowed herself to remember—there was no one to tell: not a physician, a friend, or family remained—no one safe enough or above the confines of the law to disclose to without the promise of her incarceration instead of her perpetrator's.

***

She felt crippling stabs of indescribable pain from her neck and throughout her spine, sending flares down the backs of her thighs and through the soles of her feet. Standing was doable for short bouts of time, sitting offered no relief, and lying down left her body still writhing in agony. Sleepless nights bled into days and blurred together.

Late one July evening, Hope blew out a grapefruit infused candle before her journey and fastened her home with care. One couple in her father's Rhode Island church family, Amy and Paul Gideon, extended their arms and lives to offer Hope a ride to the orthopedic spine section of the hospital that night, and other specialists to follow when her physical pain became unbearable and debilitating, allowing her to finally confront the physical aftermath of Corbin's ruthless beatings and strangulations.

That first night, Hope was met by Dr. Sato, a surgeon on call, as Mr. and Mrs. Gideon waited in wafts of hand sanitizer, confusion, and worry for their goddaughter, Hope, who had earlier lain curled in a ball of agony in the backseat of their early 2000s SUV, unable to move during their careful journey to the hospital.

From where she lay curled in agony on the gurney, Hope saw only glimpses— Amy's face pale beneath the fluorescents, Paul's hands clenched at his sides. Their lips moved, perhaps in prayer, but she couldn't hear a word over the roar in her ears filled with the constant hum of tinnitus. The nurses pushed her quickly through triage, the cold hallway tiles flashing by beneath her. Her body trembled as the stretcher rolled to a stop, and she was moved to the hospital bed beneath her that received her like a stranger. From what seemed to be jolts in just the ride down the corridors, being transferred from one bed to the next, and too many years and sleepless nights of unchecked injuries, tears leaked from Hope's eyes without sound. The pain moved through her in brutal pulses—like glowing rods shoved between her ribs and throughout her spine, radiating down her back to her legs and feet. Hope bit her lip, unsure whether the sobs were from this moment or all the ones before it, having forced herself to forget why and how she had become so debilitated and curled, moving onto her sides in a ball from the gag order issued by the judge and Corbin's torrents of wrath that had been normalized over those sixteen long years of marriage.

**

In her state, a nurse led the Gideons through her intake process on her behalf. The couple, Paul and Amy Gideon, were able to describe what Hope could not. At the bottom of her intake chart, in bold letters, it read:

DOMESTIC VIOLENCE VICTIM

But nowhere else in her voluminous medical record was that truth reflected. Hope's mind, still shackled by the influence of Corbin's intermediaries in the Mormon Church—and Judge Bullock's gag order—could not speak it. It was the Gideons alone who ensured that crucial phrase appeared at all.

Dr. Sato, the examining physician, ordered X-rays. The results were harrowing: ruptured discs in Hope's lower and mid-spine, three eroded discs in her neck—all needing surgical replacement, if not fusions. Yet even as the scans laid bare parts the skeletal trauma, the expert surgeon and pain management expert noted:

"...I do not understand why she is in such significant pain. I remain doubtful that surgery alone will resolve her level of pain; she may need to be seen in my adjacent practice for pain management with Dr. Angelino's supervision..."

That night, Hope returned to her father's home with the Gideons, who stayed by her side. Paul and Amy nursed their best friend's daughter with the tenderness they would have shown their own, had they ever had the chance. Amy, who once filled her days raising three boys, had long harbored quiet prayers for a daughter. In the past seven months, Hope—and her children, Jemma and Fowley—had become like the daughter and grandchildren she had once only dreamed of. Jonesy, Hope's father, had been Paul's close friend for as long as either could remember, deepening the bond.

Once home, they eased Hope into a freshly made bed and waited downstairs with pot after pot of coffee for themselves, as Hope would not drink any, bracing for the doctor's full diagnosis. When allowed, they tended to her pain with alternating heat and cool packs, always careful to respect the boundaries of what she could bear. In her struggle, Hope dug her nails into her flesh in failed, marked attempts to self-mitigate her pain when all else failed.

After losing her father and her children, Hope received a call that might have shattered a less numbed soul. A sister friend—Melissa Sims, wife of a member of the Bishopric—reached out in a panic. Brother Sims had struck Melissa that afternoon, knocking her unconscious, and fled with their three children to the home of Melissa's only blood sibling—another Bishop. In his possession was the last of her savings: $50,000, earned over years of teaching first grade. Left penniless, without sick leave or vacation days, Melissa faced the necessity of returning to her job to care for others' children while grieving the loss of her own.

Hope listened but could offer no comfort. Her numbness ran too deep. Uncharacteristically, she offered no words of sympathy, not even the faintest echo of encouragement. When the call ended, she simply advised Melissa to keep in touch and offered what little she had: safety tips learned in the Rhode Island shelter. Perhaps Melissa could find a similar brochure in California, maybe at a local women's group. Then Hope ended the call.

There were no words of faith or hope left to offer. She was drowning in her own unraveling reality, unable to conjure what no longer lived in her.

Hope's departure into Mormonism—or The Church of Jesus Christ of Latter-day Saints—nearly broke her father Joseph's heart.

Corbin, her husband, had thrown away the years of letters Jonesy had written to his daughter and had apparently not passed along voicemails, severing their relationship until the day she returned to her childhood home. In discarding those letters, Corbin had also destroyed Hope's father's carefully amassed knowledge mailed to his only daughter as warning signs of Mormonism—rebranded as "The Church of Jesus-Christ of Latter Day- Saints," a failed attempt to drop "Latter-Day Saints" in 2023, preferring instead to simply, but erroneously call themselves just "The Church of Jesus Christ," after an out-of-court settlement with the SEC **for hoarding roughly one Hundred Billion dollars in illegal shell corporations that allegedly made their non taxable worth rival the fourth largest Hedge fund in the United States at the time of their five million dollar Settlement with the SEC in 2023.**

***

Neither Paul nor his wife Amy knew the extent of Jonesy's encounters with "The Church" or the depth of understanding he had amassed and tucked safely in his family Bible behind a stone by the foot of the fireplace after Hope was woven into the folds of this powerful political strongarm. They were unaware of the toll her father and their dear friend had quietly borne, the private battles he had fought when his daughter began getting pulled back into that community through fear and control tactics. Only Joseph Livingston himself had borne witness to this descent, tracking it obsessively through news clippings, notepads, printed-out emails, and carefully dated, filed documents. In these private writings were laid out the differences between the Church of the Godmakers—once called Mormons, now conveniently rebranded "The Church of Jesus Christ of Latter-day

Saints"— a body that manipulated and drained life from his daughter and grandchildren, rather than revealing to them the unfathomable love, grace, mercy, and sheer joy of the Father and Creator of all things. This Heavenly Father had offered His only Son as the Messiah, the final peace and Passover offering for the sins of the first humans who disobeyed and forced Him, through their willful disobedience and pride, to slaughter one of His creatures to clothe them before their exodus from Eden into a broken world—fallen in their sin—the Christian belief in Original Sin; contrary to LDS/Mormon teachings of Original Godmaker design. This truth had not been lost on Hope. She had learned it through her father, through the Gideons, and their pastor. A truth incomprehensible to human love: that the Creator of all things still beckons all who would believe in His Son's name, offering life and salvation through grace and faith alone. That access to God is found only through His Son in human form, who submitted Himself to death on a cross meant for criminals, taking upon Himself all He abhorred—sins, sickness, every imperfection that separates creation from the Father who sent Him.

His resurrection and ascension three days later were not myth but history— attested to by eyewitnesses, archaeology, and the historical record. The Son, the Messiah, had walked the earth, suffered not for the perfect but for the broken, and He was, and is, and is to come: the Redeemer, the only way back to the God who sent Him. This revelation remains open to all who seek in humble need and is revealed by the One whom the Father sent after His Son's ascension—named by some the Holy Spirit—who is omnipresent, omniscient, and omnipotent; and 180 degrees different in Nature, Doctrine, and Practice from the "jesus christ," of the ever-rebranding Mormon Political/ Corporate Organization that cries wolf about being labeled a "religious, tax – exempt entity," by its Presidents.

As Hope lay broken in every way, beneath the colorful hand-stitched floral, horse, and other quilts her father had decorated her room with, the Gideon family left faint songs to pour over their God-daughter—especially *Defender* by Rita Springer, *House of Miracles* (extended version) by Brandon Lake, *Tend*, and others by Emmy Rose, Elevation Worship, Leeland, We the Kingdom, Maverick City Music, and other Christian musical artists familiar to her father and his church family, like Amy and Paul Gideon. This couple did everything in their power to tether Hope to healing in her stifled grief with offerings of new and familiar songs, their prayers, and wordless, selfless acts of that indescribable love ascribed to their Jesus of the Holy Bible—the same love her father had embodied during his life. Until Hope's MRIs came back, Amy and Paul cared for her like their own daughter. Hope was given nerve-blocking pain reliever pills that did not do much good. Something inside her had long ago learned to shift her personality to ignore pain and please others. Around people she knew, their happiness often exceeded her own need. So her mind silenced her agony while they were there. Another aftermath of the layer upon layer of Corbin's types and years of abuse was the erasure of Hope's identity—beginning with the first of many lashes from his belt, demanding her to count and thank him for this unwanted and unneeded education.

He supplemented these "lessons" with others his hands and body delivered to her physiology whenever she displeased him, across sixteen long, physical years of married life.

It was only to her physicians and their attendants that Hope ever revealed snippets of the fullness of her pain, the aftermath of years she'd gagged her mind from remembering. Corbin's acts upon her had long been normalized, dismissed, or rationalized by those who knew them both.

The California Bishop, his counselors, Stake Presidencies, and the Patriarch were there to watch from the outside in—silent witnesses to the hurricanes of beatings across her torso, the strangulations, the stillborn children whom the Bishop whisked away as "non-viable pregnancies, Hope.

Oh, those are not your children. Their spirits were returned to our Heavenly Parents beyond the veil; for them to be born to a different, more worthy earthly family. They will not know you, nor will you see them in the Celestial Kingdom.

They will go to different Forever Families, now."

***

Neither Amy nor Paul knew the full extent of what Hope's father taught himself about The Church of Jesus Christ of Latter-day Saints, or Mormons. So, when Hope's local Ward members began trickling by—having heard rumors that Hope was due for surgery—and brought carefully prepared meals, words of encouragement, cards, and heartfelt prayers, the Gideons felt supported. They believed Hope was in good hands. After all, these visitors attended a place they called "The Church of Jesus Christ of Latter-day Saints" and claimed to be Christians. So wouldn't they believe in the same Christ as other Christians, and not in a "Heavenly Father who is confined to live on a planet he created called Kolob; just one in an endless eternal line of 'Heavenly Fathers?" Didn't sound Christian to Jonesy.

Innocently, the Gideons opened Hope's refuge and home to an extension of the very same marauders who had erased her father's faith, her memories, and irreplaceable decades of her life. They had orchestrated the legal maneuverings that kidnapped her children, and they now threatened her eternal security with the Savior of her father—and her newfound rock, the one true Messiah—by reintroducing familiar but different pawns who served up confusion and heartbreak alongside casserole dishes, melty chocolate chip cookies, and warm cinnamon-sprinkled snickerdoodles.

The bitter pill, repeated from the President of the International Organization—the one in which Hope and Corbin had not truly been remarried but rather *sealed for time and* eternity—refused to recognize their state and U.S.-legally recognized divorce. A letter echoed the former decree:

"What has once been sealed for time and all eternity cannot, will not be unsealed, lest you (Hope) are eternally separated from not only the children you shamefully lost your mother's right to care for on Earth through your failure to reconcile your union with your eternal companion and husband..."

And so, slowly, members of the Church of Jesus Christ of Latter-day Saints— or the local Mormon ward—bled through her father's former bastion and back into Hope's life, invading her sanctuary with the comforting fragrance of homemade cinnamon rolls and banana bread, laced with misleading, confusing doctrines and histories of bloody betrayals.

The presidential admonishment went on to state that the **only** way to break the sealing bonds to Corbin *might* be possible *if* Hope were to fall in love with a temple-worthy Mormon man, and *if* she were to request a cancellation of sealing from Corbin—who had every right to refuse without cause. But *if* Corbin consented, and *if* Hope were to go through the temple ordinances again and become sealed anew to a different Latter-day Saint, then she could dwell in the afterlife with Christ, Heavenly Father, and be reunited with Jemma and Fowley, her own father, and others who had passed away.

But only if she remained loyal to the Church.

Corbin had faked his offer to divorce and reconcile, and Hope's father had ensured that reconciliation was out of the question.

Hope tasted the tang of her own blood in her mouth as she read the words in the First President's letter:

"Only under those rare circumstances could Hope's eternity with Corbin be 'canceled,' and Hope was further instructed that if she did the unthinkable and left 'The Church of Jesus Christ'—otherwise known as The One True Church on Earth, or the Mormon or Latter-day Saint organization—that she would be committing the unforgivable sin of violating the Holy Ghost and would be banished to the lowest level of exaltation—none.

No hell for her, but stricken from the minds and hearts of all her loved ones for eternity, and banished forever from the presence of

their non-Biblical Jesus and no Heavenly Father for her or others like her— banished to 'Outer Darkness,' adrift in voiceless cold and solitude."

***

Hope felt like a gutted melon that had been discarded, then repurposed and stuffed with raw, rancid, rotting, hot, festering hamburger meat where her heart and insides had once been. Stitched up on the outside, with a forced smile affixed that was unable to be removed, lest all of her stitches come apart and the wrong things shoved inside her spill out: uncontainable, visible, misjudged, and irreparably exposed in the midday sun for anyone to poke and squish.

It took three years for Hope to obtain the pain-mitigating surgeries she required to sustain her life. Until then, she managed with cocktails of medication to silence the flaming stabs of nerve pain once they arrived at her brain, coupled with medication recommended by her doctor and psychiatrist to mitigate her involuntary spikes in anxiety and deep layers of depression **associated with a diagnosis recognized by the World Health Organization as Complex Post-Traumatic Stress Disorder, but not** differentiated by the academic authorities in the United States from singular PTSD.

Amy and Paul Gideon had long since removed Hope and her father's

"BEWARE Of DOG!"

sign, not understanding its significance or reference, after re-homing her dad's dog, as Hope lay in one bout of crippling pain after another, unable to think or tend to daily tasks around the house.

When the sign was removed, it was as if checkered flags were furiously waved to signal a

"COME ON IN!!!"

invitation to the sister missionaries and other women from the Church of Jesus Christ of Latter-day Saints to stream by and into Hope's empty life, offering flickers of friendship with potential suitors, "once Hope felt up to it."

One fellow single sister offered to arrange a flight and hotel stay in two rooms at an opulent chain of luxurious hotels owned by a prestigious Mormon family to attend a national singles event in Las Vegas.

"Awe, it'll be fun! You don't have to dance or anything; I never do. But you… they will be lining up to take you to a chapel!" the sister laughed.

Hope was not familiar with the word "chapel" being used in the Mormon dialect in relation to anything except for Sunday meeting houses, "the chapel" section being the initial gathering place for hymns and lay sermons, void of any ornamentation, cross, or reverence point, except for the height-adjustable podium with a handful of chairs adjacent to it and a few choir pews behind those chairs, reserved for the local presiding bishop and his counselors.

The sister giggled,

"Oh, Hope! No! What happens in Vegas stays in Vegas! There are wedding chapels open round the clock. I mean, what's the harm in trying out the union before a temple sealing for all of eternity? Ew! No, out there we're free to hop to a chapel, have a honeymoon, and if that doesn't work, well, annulments happen there, too! No ex-spouse, no harm; just trial runs before the temple leap. What do you say?"

Hope was stunned as she asked the sister to further explain this whole chapel- jumping process, feeling her gut wrench at what she wanted to block out about what she was hearing.

"Is this what it's reduced to?" Hope thought as the sister continued.

This "trying out" of potential spouses in bed, or who knows how many 'tryouts' before ever meeting a man who loved her from the inside out—and not because of her exterior—sickened Hope, and she declined the sister's generous offer.

***

Hope preferred the solitude, journaling, and delving into the Christian books and songs her father and the Gideons had introduced her to that played such a significant role in her healing.

Hope was invited to attend a special Saturday meeting by the sisters at the local ward, and feeling worn down from many months of refusing their invitations, she went, just to appease them.

When she walked with the sister missionaries into the main room of the meetinghouse and the chapel, floodgates of awful memories mixed with what she thought were fond ones rushed through her senses. She grabbed the wooden pew beside her and caught her breath before the sisters ushered her near the front of the room, sitting between them so she could not leave without causing a scene.

It seemed that even in her soul sickness, Hope had impressed the guest speaker for some reason and was asked to stay after the meeting with the Sisters, her "companions," who both guarded her escape and drove her there. While Hope waited, she busied herself washing the silverware, plates, and plastic water pitchers that had been brought back to the kitchen, all the while wearing a sincere smile. She was happy to serve in small ways and listened to the other Sisters talk about their lives, families, and ward business as if she were someone outside herself. The women there had known Jemma and Fowley, and some even remembered her father, so no one asked Hope about her life, which comforted her with a sense of cordial respect. Later, Hope would learn that the Sisters had left without telling her. They drove to their apartment to meet their curfew, leaving her to hitch a ride or take a long walk back home.

Soon, Hope was among the last few people in the building as she dried the last serving spoons and hung the white and sunny yellow towel after her work. Suddenly, a silver-haired, keen-eyed man in grey striped suit pants, with his jacket folded over his left arm, swung open the brown wooden kitchen door and asked Hope if she needed help taking out the large black bin of garbage before Sunday's services the next morning. His speckled green eyes danced as he leaned over and lifted the garbage out of the can. His eyes darted back to meet hers as he asked her to wait for him to return.

"Who is this man?"

Hope thought silently as she unfolded a large black bag to replace the full one that this stranger had just taken outside to the bin.

He reappeared through the door, a gust of cool winter air helping to close it behind him. As the man strode over and began scrubbing his hands in the stainless steel sink Hope had just cleaned, Brother James Richardson beamed at her while he talked and joked, his green eyes sparkling and his wide smile lingering long after his hands were cleaned and dried. He drew Hope into light conversation.

He later quipped, "What's a gal like you doing in a place like this? Would you join me for a late-night slice of pie? Or dessert, if you know of any place that's open? You're a lady I'd like to get to know, if that's all right?"

Hope smiled and asked for the time, then laughed along with Brother Richardson when they realized it was past 11 at night.

"I'm sorry, but I don't know of any places open this late. When Jemma—" Hope caught her breath at the vivid memories of her daughter's late-night cries soon after exiting the shelter, when she whined for comfort in ice cream. This had been a long-standing joke between Hope and her father, as her requests were softly denied and bedtime stories replaced sweets.

Hope returned to the present as Brother Richardson looked at her, expecting her to finish her sentence, which had now become more than a pregnant pause.

"Oh, I'm sorry! This time has flown by, Brother Richardson. I don't know of any place open this late here."

"Well, Sister Livingston, may I give you my phone number? You are still a lady I'd like to learn more about," Brother Richardson continued. "You are unmarried, and so am I. Is my information correct?"

Hope laughed involuntarily. "Yes, who told you?" His green eyes grew soft as he replied, "Sister Livingston, that's why I'm here. I think. I received a call to be here for the presentation tonight about a month ago. Are you tired? Do you need to go?"

Hope's mind raced, her heart pounding. "What does he mean, 'that's why he's here and he received a call?'"

"Brother Richardson, yes, I am tired, to be honest, but I am now more curious than tired. Please, will you explain?"

He suggested they close up the kitchen and sit in the foyer, in more comfortable surroundings. Hope shuddered at the thought of the plump velvet maroon chair awaiting her as she flicked on the hall and foyer lights and made her way down the hall before sinking into the welcoming folds of the soft cushions. Her nerves had been burned out throughout her spine earlier in the year, and she had undergone surgery in her mid and lower back the year before. Only neck surgery remained, and this round of pain management would be finished until her nerves grew back in a year or two and would need to be ablated again. This would be her self-care regimen for the rest of her life, she mused, as feelings of overwhelming gratitude welled up within her for the physicians who had saved her life in so many ways.

"Sister Livingston, if it is appropriate, you may call me Jim, like any of my colleagues or friends."

Jim went on to describe his position and a higher priesthood calling in the Church that was being considered. As a fairly new convert with a long career leading to tenured experience as a National Consultant Health Physicist, specializing in the determination, assurance, monitoring, and oversight of safety and radiation standards for both patients and healthcare staff, Jim had spent his life focused on his career. He mentioned that he had married early and soon divorced due to the demands of his work, leaving him with five adult children from his first marriage, whom he rarely saw as they were all busy with their own lives, careers, and families. After joining the Church, Jim said he had been "tapped" for higher callings, which he didn't receive because he remained unmarried.

Jim sat opposite Hope, his white dress shirt still crisp, his black Italian shoe tips glossed under the warm light in the waiting area adjacent to the chapel. As he leaned toward her, his right ankle resting on his left knee, his grey and black pinstriped pant leg still creased from Hope's view, his arms shifted on the plush wingback chair. He planted both feet on the tannish Berber carpet and leaned in closer to Hope, a sliver of hair falling out of his intentionally groomed part, now hung like a side bang feathering half of his face.

"Sister, you haven't told me your first name, although I have told you mine. After the presentation tonight, during the gathering, I noticed no ring on your lovely wedding finger, but a slight indentation where one may have once been. One aspect that drew me to the Church was the emphasis on wholesome family values and The Family Proclamation to the World, with high standards, which my first marriage lacked."

Jim lowered his head as Hope remained silent, then continued. "I would love to find my other half. I've lived for it. A bright woman who has likely made mistakes like I did in my youth, not a cradle-raised member. I think you might also want something, as we've stayed here now past 1 in the morning, and you've not left, but laughed at my corny jokes, and your smile…"

Jim's voice trailed off, and Hope spoke as if to save him from drowning. "Please call me Hope, Jim. Yes, please call me Hope."

His emerald eyes shimmered as he looked back up at her.

Hope laughed. "You are right that it is now past 1, and it's morning, and here we are."

Her tone grew somber as her mind shifted from this fleeting moment to her layers of loss and the importance of children and families in the Church.

"How can I possibly begin to explain losing Jemma and Fowley to such a monster?" she wavered.

She stammered,

"I...I do not know if I am a befitting wife for you," Hope concluded. Jim stood up, held out both hands to Hope, and pulled her to her feet.

"Why don't you let me decide that? If you give me your phone, I will give you my number. Maybe we can go have breakfast later this afternoon?"

Hope laughed and agreed but then stopped herself.

"Jim, I just cannot be hurt or let anyone else get hurt. If you are looking for a wife who can bear you children, then..."

Hope's mind went back to the STD Corbin had gifted her before or during her pregnancy with Fowley, which had gone undiagnosed and untreated for far too long, leaving her barren, according to three OBs in the Church.

"If you want children, then I...I...we can't."

Jim's face softened as he brushed Hope's jawline and chin with his gentle index finger.

"I don't understand, but you can't scare me off that quickly, Hope. Go get some rest. Call me when you wake up, okay?"

"Don't cry! Not here! Not now!"

Hope pleaded with herself and nodded in agreement to Jim.

He held her coat as she put it on, then locked the meetinghouse after walking her to Paul Gideon's waiting car. He watched as they drove away.

***

Hope Livingston and James Richardson were married and sealed in an official Mormon temple ceremony in Boston, attended by friends from Rhode Island who knew Hope, as well as many others there to congratulate Jim and welcome Hope as his Eternal Companion; wife to a High Priest for whom Heavenly Father had great aspirations. While this new union severed Hope's eternal ties to Corbin and his family, it maintained her eternity with Jemma and Fowley, drawing her back into a life her father had worked tirelessly to extricate her from.

Neither the Gideons nor any of Hope's family-like friends, who were connected to her father or his grandchildren, were allowed to attend the Temple marriage or Sealing Ceremony of the Mormon/ "Church of Jesus Christ of Latter-Day Saints." As the living prophets and presidents say, "Not because it's a secret, but because it's sacred." Is that what Joseph Smith said, too, about burning his Brother's printing press to hide his other 30 wives from his wife, Emma, and his followers? What DID happen to false prophets in the Old Testament? Did any of Joseph Smith's curses upon his killers come true? Hope pondered these questions as long as she could whilst forced underwater to drown; as she felt her relationship with Paul and Amy Gideon and her Father's extended Christian family sever under the sanctity of a spiritual hacksaw with the Temple Sealing. She forgot as she was allowed up for air, by her new husband, Jim.

Ah, such bliss! To be clean from her sins and un-Sealed from Corbin, yes?

***

Author's Note

Identity theft doesn't always involve a stolen name—it can be the slow, silent erasure of a person's worth, agency, and future. This isn't just a personal tragedy; it's a systemic collapse that allows abusers to rewrite the lives of their victims.

According to the National Coalition Against Domestic Violence, **1 in 3 women** will experience physical violence in their lifetime (NCADV, 2019), and the trauma inflicted on children in these homes is both vast and invisible.

As you walk with Hope through her devastation, **ask yourself:** *What is the one legal or societal reform you would fight for to protect children who cannot protect themselves?*

Let that question ignite something deeper than sympathy—**let it spark action**. Because every time we fail to act, another child's voice, future, and identity is silenced.

(**Alliance for Hope, 2020;** *Divine Theft***, 2025**)

Chapter 10

Child(ren) Erased - 18 Years Through Last Winter

Roughly seven months after their Temple sealing—in Jim's house in Maine, which he had purchased as a wedding gift not just for his second wife, but for Jemma, Fowley, and his own adult children and

their families whenever they visited—Hope noticed how the shadows stretched long and thin through the windows. The house never truly felt like it belonged to her, even if it bore her name in some buried legal record.

When she and Jim married, they clearly hadn't expected more children. But when their first of seven arrived, Hope's heart swelled with joy at what seemed to be a miraculous healing. Jim's stony heart and logical mind did not follow Hope's. His jagged responses to each child's conception and throughout their lives echoed in her memory, and shattered throughout their children's minds like shrapnel.

"I thought these were supposed to be our Golden Years! You just married me so you could have a kid —well, you've got them now, Hope! They are YOURS. Now leave me alone!"

Jim said those blameshifting scapegoating words so often they etched themselves into her stifled mind—and even worse, into the hearts and spirits of their children, whom Jim had no problem siring. Despite his rebukes for Hope to "leave him alone," Jim didn't seem to leave her alone long enough to allow her to breathe between children or to take contraception seriously for himself. Hope soon saw that lust and hubris lurked in the shadows behind closed doors after their sealing was complete, and it was too late to undo. Long before their eldest child Emma's birth, Hope sensed it; she felt the familiar dread in a different way from Corbin, in a similar "Be Thou perfect for Thee, oh—but not for Me," hidden beneath another marriage facade with a different man. Jim didn't lay a hand on his wife or children until later, much like Corbin's assaults on his first wife began by reducing Hope to a rag doll, hearing her sobs over a pack of gum.

Jim's smile, when it came, was like a test—soft enough to pass as tender, but Hope quickly learned to read the sharpness beneath. "*A virtuous wife suffers long,*" he'd told her in the beginning, his voice low with reverent conviction. "*Only the meek shall inherit.*" Sometimes he withheld a simple gesture—a plate of toast, a kind word—just long enough to remind her who held control. He didn't have to shout or strike. His discipline was quieter, more precise. And crueler. Some mornings, she even found herself wondering if maybe he was right—that she was just too sensitive, too emotional. That frightened her the most.

More children came after Emma. Leo was born just under a year later, followed by Sebastian two years after Leo. By the time of Anna's birth, near Hope's 43rd birthday, she had grown accustomed to hearing how the sound of their children, the meals she'd prepared to Jim's specifications, and even the weather somehow fell short of Jim's and their "Heavenly Parents' Standards."

Alongside these words, Jim hurled others, jagged and sharp-edged like glass:

"If you don't like it, there's the door, Hope. Take YOUR kids and go."

Hope witnessed how those cruel refrains became the foundation of her children's memories. Jim never raised a hand like Corbin had, but the things he said—God, they cut deeper than fists ever could. And though he'd told her to leave him alone, he rarely practiced what he preached. Two years after Anna, the twins Matthew and Molly arrived, followed by Samuel— testimony to how he desired to pass the time. Hope asked about getting her tubes tied but was met with a cold, indifferent refusal from her husband, rivaling an indigo-tinged lightning-white wall of ice bricks.

When Jim's adult children or Jemma and Fowley visited, a darker ritual unfolded. Jim would displace his children and Hope's from their rooms, pushing them to the sofas and sleeping bags in the living room, sometimes handing their toys or belongings over to his older children and grandchildren like disposable relics. Hope felt it in her chest every time— an invisible stab, multiplied by the confusion and silenced betrayal in her children's eyes. If she tried to leave their bed to comfort her youngest children by sleeping nearby, Jim simply occupied her until she was physically too raw to move.

Jim's cruelty wasn't loud or bloody. It was quiet and systematic. He ruled the home like a master, and every child—even the youngest—seemed to hold their breath in his presence.

She remembered their first two years when Emma and Leo were babies. Back then, Jim had poured himself into legal battles for Jemma and Fowley, sparing no expense—attorneys, expert witnesses, long drives back and forth to Boston. Hope, tired and heavy with grief, held those babies in her arms while still fighting for her oldest children in court. Jim had even once wanted to adopt Jemma and Fowley to protect them, but as the years passed and they returned from Corbin's care full of rage and mistrust, that window of hope shut tight, and any remaining softness in Jim's heart toward his wife and their children permanently petrified. Hope became an outlet for his insatiable lust, and their children became scapegoats for any of his woes.

When things soured with Jemma and Fowley, Jim didn't grieve the loss. Instead, he adjusted—shifting blame onto Hope and their children. She began to notice just two years into their marriage how people at The Church grew stiff around her, overly polite or oddly distant.

She realized then that Jim had planted the seeds early—quiet whispers to the bishopric, carefully chosen words about her "fragile state" and "emotional strain," in hushed tones to the Relief Society Presidency and female leadership that she overheard; stunned and stung. He cloaked his betrayals in the language of spiritual concern. "We're just worried about her," he had said. The effect was isolation. Former acquaintances she might have befriended in another town kept their distance. The Relief Society sisters stopped including her in activities. She wasn't just lonely—she'd been spiritually quarantined. All contact with her friends in Rhode Island severed since the Temple sealing.

At first, she blamed herself. But gradually, she realized: Jim had been laying the groundwork. *"Hope's not quite well,"* he'd once said within earshot of the babysitter's parents after Leo's birth. *"A bit fragile."* Subtle discrediting, offered with concern, as if protecting her from herself. The fact that her closest friendships never took root in this town suddenly made sense. Jim didn't just want distance—he manufactured it.

From the outside, Jim looked like a calm, successful man—a respected engineer. But inside the walls of their home, Hope saw the fractures daily.

Her children's cries were muffled, yes, but never silent. Their grief lived in hushed sobs and nervous laughter. Hope often stood in the middle of it all, torn between the ghosts of the past and the children of the present.

On those summer visits, when Jemma and Fowley were in the house, the air shifted. They carried Corbin's cruelty with them like second skin, their eyes sharp, their movements charged. Yet, even through that darkness, Hope occasionally glimpsed the children they had once been—warm, tender, capable of kindness. Those flickers never lasted.

One afternoon, a sudden fight erupted. Fowley, frustrated, struck Jemma across the face. Jemma responded with animalistic fury, biting his leg and drawing blood. Hope heard it unfold—blood and vitriol in equal measure— and even when it ended, the tension bled through the household like smoke. She could see it on her younger children's faces—confused, anxious, hurt— but none of them had the words to name what they were experiencing.

Sometimes, Jemma surprised her. She'd sit gently with the twins, guiding them through coloring books with the kind of soft patience Hope wished she could rely on. But it never lasted long. That sweetness could turn into venom in an instant. Fowley, always restless, challenged Leo to bike races that left Sebastian trailing behind. Hope watched it all—her heart breaking as Fowley mocked Sebastian, calling him a "baby," as if thirteen were a stain. Even Leo, just fifteen, looked weary from the effort of trying to hold everything together.

Jim never disguised his preference. His loyalty to Jemma and Fowley, and to Corbin's unspoken hold, remained fixed. His coldness toward his own children with Hope—a look, a silence, a scornful word—became an odd daily ritual.

One evening, Hope watched Jim slip silently through the back door toward the machinist shop he had built for himself on the property—a cold sentinel disappearing into his world of blueprints and tools. She imagined what he thought as he walked away: calculated, distant, and empty of remorse.

Later that night, she dared to step inside the shop, not intending to be so silent as she followed him. He hadn't seen her. He stood over his workbench, holding something carefully in his hand—it was Anna's birthday card, the one with carefully drawn red crayon hearts and glitter glue smudged across the front. He turned it slowly in his fingers, then, without a blink, crumpled it into the wastebasket among a pile of his bent nails and broken screws; as if the card and his daughter who made it were both disposable garbage pieces that didn't belong. Hope didn't confront him; she simply backed away and stood in the hallway, her heart cracking. That image stuck with her forever— not the discard, but his deliberation.

She had caught glimpses of his dehumanization in his face, that smooth exterior which once promised safety, now hardened with indifference.

She could only guess at his detachment, but she saw it reflected in Anna's growing silence, her fire. At ten, Anna already spoke in narrowed eyes and clenched fists—the language of quiet resistance to layered betrayals.

Hope sometimes overheard whispers in Leo and Sebastian's room. One night, she paused in the hallway. Behind the cracked door, she heard Sebastian's voice, low and cracking.

"I hate it here. Not because of you guys—just him. I hate how he looks at us." Leo's voice followed, steady. "We're not staying forever."

Then Anna, whispering fiercely, "Next time he makes that face at me, I'll punch him. I swear, I will."

Hope hadn't dared enter. She backed away, tears pricking her eyes—not because they were angry, but because they were right. They were forming their own lifeboat in the storm. She didn't always know the content, but she recognized the cadence of secrets and survival. She felt it palpably in Leo. At fifteen, he bore too much—an unspoken vow to protect them all amidst what seemed to be a shadow of his own burdens. Hope ached with guilt over her oldest son's burdens that were not his to bear alone. She tried to reach him, but in some ways, pride had overtaken him; he couldn't or wouldn't receive help from her. She had seen the way Jim praised his older children and those firstborns from his earlier life, casting a dismissive glance over Emma, Leo, Sebastian, and Anna—all the others. They were hers, but they were his too. Why couldn't he see them?

Some nights, she lay awake listening to the silence between the clanks of Jim's machines. She imagined that somewhere beneath the whirring metal and precise measurements, there might still be something human left in him. But if there was, he buried it too deep.

Maybe he had once felt guilt. Maybe not. She didn't know anymore. What she did know was this: the children saw through him. They saw every act of dismissal, every stolen affection. And though they didn't yet have the words to name their pain, Hope did. She carried it in her heart.

She would not forget. And someday, she prayed, neither would they; that this cycle would end.

*****

This video call with Fowley and Jemma brought it all rushing back. It hadn't been the first time.

There had been a summer just after Sammy's first birthday when Jemma had taken control of the phone during an unsupervised but recorded court-mandated video call with Fowley. Her tone had been syrupy and coaxing.

"Let's go on a trip," she told the twins, Matthew and Molly, just five years old at the time.

Hope found them in the hallway, dragging overnight bags stuffed with socks, stuffed animals, and even a soup ladle.

"Jemma said to wait by the stairs," Molly whispered. "She's coming to get us."

Hope had grabbed the phone just in time to hear Jemma's final instruction:

"Once everyone's upstairs, I'll scream. Then the bags will trip them on the way down."

It wasn't a prank; it was a blueprint for chaos—and it was almost executed.

Hope had shut it down fast, but the chill never left her. After that, the speakerphone and Hope's presence in the room became mandatory. So did therapy.

When she grabbed the phone, she heard the calculated stillness in Jemma's voice. Her daughter had grown razor-sharp, almost unrecognizable.

"You don't get to manipulate my children," Hope had said, barely able to keep her voice from trembling. "Until you can speak to me like a person I once knew—someone I can trust—you are not welcome in this household."

Jemma had exploded.

"I'll call Jim! He sides with me! You're just a mean bitch like always. I wish Dad had killed you when he had the chance!"

Then the line went dead.

Afterward, Hope had soothed the children and scheduled counseling. She set a new rule: all of the Court mandated phone calls would be on speaker, with witnesses. But the fear lingered.

And now, seeing Jemma's face again, hearing that same lilt of manipulation... it hit differently. This time, the danger felt closer.

Hope stood frozen as the phone screen went black. The room was silent except for the quiet breathing of her children gathered close. It wasn't the threat of two wayward adults that struck her—it was the certainty. The precision. This was a legacy passed down through whispered instructions and twisted love and loyalty to one who hated all of them.

On the screen just moments before, Jemma had stood with wild conviction in her flashing eyes. Her voice had turned low and venomous.

"You think you can escape us, Mom? Look at me. We're better than Dad ever was. He taught us. And so did MeMaw."

Then Fowley had stepped in, his voice cold and flat, no longer belonging to the child she once knew.

"Remember the pipe bombs, Mom? Remember how fast people can disappear? No threats, just promises. What's yours is ours—just like Dad said."

The words weren't just threats—they were rehearsed oaths, generational legacies of control. Hope had felt the air go thin, as if the house itself recoiled.

Jim's voice from years past cut through the fog in her mind like a knife and suddenly broke the silence.

"Use your head and think! Are you stupid? If you don't like it, there's the door!"

Hope blinked, jolted back. For the first time in decades, she saw it clearly. No more passivity. No more waiting. She would teach her children what she had spent too long learning.

"Emma, Leo, Sebastian, Anna, Molly, Matthew, Sammy," she said, her voice steady. "What did you hear on that call? When's the last time you spoke with Jemma or Fowley?"

She waited. She wouldn't lead them—just listen. Matthew and Molly clung to her sides.

"Mommy, they scared us," Matthew whispered. "Are they coming here?" Sebastian looked up, his face pale.

"Fowley threw me in the air. Like a ball. Lifted me like weights. When was that?"

Hope did the math—over three years ago for Fowley, even longer since Jemma. A chill ran through her, deeper than just the call. Corbin hadn't just taken her children—he had been rewarded for it. She remembered discovering the Social Security statements: her ex-husband receiving dependent benefits from the government based on the very disabilities he had inflicted on her. He got paid for her broken spine, her surgeries, her pain. And all the while, she scraped together change for school supplies while his children posted photos from Disneyland. That kind of injustice didn't scream; it bled slowly, methodically, until you just went blank.

She suddenly remembered the court filings, the recordings, the documentation. After more than a decade of marriage and over a decade and a half of supposed co-parenting—Corbin was still pulling strings—through the children she had never let go of and through love and fear for them—not a thought for herself.

This mother now spoke slowly, deliberately choosing every word wisely and purposefully.

"I don't know where they are. But maybe that's not the question. Where are we? What do we have that they don't?"

The children fell silent, deep in thought. Anna's voice broke the silence.

"What did they mean about erasing people? You can't just erase a person… can you?"

Hope looked at her daughter for a long moment.

"Some people try," she said softly. "They pretend something never happened or ensure no one is left who remembers it did.

It's not magic—it's control. And fear." She swallowed hard. "And it works… until someone refuses to forget."

Hope's mind churned, replaying Jemma's and Fowley's words.

She didn't know where they were, but deep inside, she sensed they knew exactly where she and her children were. And she knew where they were headed; with as much certainty as Corbin had when he had his legal filings drafted, as Jemma acted out while her father restrained her before his death. Jemma was far too old for a timeout. They had never worked with Fowley, except when Jim initiated them. These two were adults now; any reprimand Hope could offer would be like futile thrashing in the grasp of a boa constrictor.

Her father's old house, the one she had offered to the church as a shelter for fleeing mothers, flickered in her memory.

Leo spoke next, his tone grave.

"Yeah, Anna… I think some people can be erased. fowley said it for years. Pipe bombs. Kill everyone we know. Mom, should we call the police?"

The front door creaked open. Jim stepped inside, brushing snow off his jacket. He caught Leo's question and barked a laugh.

"Call the police? for what? I'm not scared of Corbin. He'd be laughing right now too! And if you don't like it, you know where the door is."

Hope didn't look at him. She wasn't thinking about Corbin anymore.

She was thinking about her children—and how to save them from their father's legacy. And what she suddenly realized were Corbin's children; since the moment she'd left him; and maybe before, not hers— living evidence of his promises— not threats.

***

With Jim's sort of blessing, the battlefield now set amidst the tangled vines of history and heartbreak and the thought of the cycle repeating itself, Hope resolved not to let her youngest children's light be snuffed out by shadows of familiar terror. The journey to redemption bore its unique merciless toll, and in her heart of hearts, Hope braced for the unthinkable that lay ahead as she arranged for "her kids," as Jim called them, to each pack a bag and head for the van. Hope withdrew just enough cash for gas and cheap motels after she loaded decades of her own legal and medical legacy into boxfuls in the back of the large, dark-quasar blue van Jim had relented to putting in Hope's name, along with their 12-person tent and preparations for the long wait she knew lay ahead due to grossly underfunded domestic violence shelters, typically without one spare bed, let alone several.

Before she left, something tugged at her. That night, long after the children were asleep and Jim had retreated to his machinist shop, Hope felt drawn to the attic. She hadn't been up there in years. With a flashlight in hand, she crept up the steep stairs. Her foot knocked against something wooden. She bent down and gasped—her childhood rocking horse, carved by her father's hands, its faded paint still holding the warmth of old memories.

She dropped to her knees, ran her hands along its worn handles, and let the tears come freely. Next to the horse were boxes marked simply: "Hope."

One by one, she opened them—carefully, reverently. Inside was a journal with a periwinkle cover, a birthday gift from her father before he died. As she opened the book, a note fluttered out.

"With love and grace to you, dear friend. We cannot ever love you the same way your father did, but we will love you as our own. Love always, Paul and Amy Gideon."

Before leaving the attic, Hope sat with the journal in her lap and let memory carry her deeper.

Before she'd moved to Maine, before Jim and the long unraveling, there had been a conversation. A pastor from her father's church had reached out. He was working on a new project—a missions-based shelter for women and children escaping abuse.

Hope had known what she had to do.

The house her father built with his own two hands had been her sanctuary once. It had been where she recovered from Corbin, where she wept with Jemma and Fowley in her arms, where her father held them all in his unwavering embrace. It was a home born of selfless love.

So she gave it to the church.

Not for money. Not for recognition.

Just one dollar, she told Pastor Marcus. And only if he promised to keep her name anonymous.

"This is my offering," she had said, seated across from his desk in a cold gray chair, her voice trembling. "It's the only legacy I can give in return for what he gave me."

The pastor had tried to refuse. But she insisted. And in the end, he gave her a dollar bill, crisp and folded. She kept it in her Bible for years.

Now, as she sat on the attic floor beside her childhood rocking horse, Hope closed the journal and wept anew—not just for what was lost, but for what still endured. Her father's love lived on, not in stone or siding, but in sanctuary.

Hope held the note against her chest. For the first time in a long time, she felt seen—not just as a mother or a survivor, but as Hope. That girl from

Rhode Island who once believed in kindness. She knew she would return for these boxes, but for now, she closed the lids gently, her resolve firming with each breath. What was lost might not be reclaimed, but the truth of who she was could still be remembered.

She descended the attic stairs, her heart a little heavier but her spirit steadier, and resumed packing with a clarity that hadn't been there before.

Before returning to the attic to bring the boxes to the van, Hope slipped into the upstairs hallway bathroom and quietly called Amy.

"Hope?" Amy answered quickly. "It's late. Are you all right?"

Hope held the phone close stammering, fingers trembling. "I found Dad's journal in the attic. And the rocking horse. And—your note."

A pause, then Amy's warm voice: "We meant every word."

Hope pressed the phone tighter to her ear. "Do you still have the house keys?"

"Yes. It's still in use by the shelter. But I can make calls. We'll find a way, Hope. Come home."

Hope didn't cry. She couldn't. But a breath escaped her—half relief, half grief. "Thank you."

She hung up before Jim could hear her and then moved—fast, focused—toward the next right step back to the attic to retrieve the remaining boxes and to pack the van up before the drive she would make in the morning. Her mind clear and thinking she was responding in kind without reaction.

As Hope sorted through belongings that night and memories pulled at her— a day she never wanted to revisit kept demanding her attention. The Mormon Temple ceremony. It was the second Mormon "wedding," where they Sealed her to Jim. She'd been dosed with so many pain meds from her last spinal surgery that she barely remembered it—the rustle and smoothness of her starched white gown, the heat of the oil on her scalp beneath her veil, the circle of men's hands, and the sharp slice of betrayal— because they made her believe this was God's will. That she had to be bound to a man for eternity, even after escaping the one who nearly killed her. She'd wept silently afterward in the temple dressing room, the sheer white veil bunched in hands that she could no longer form tight fists with. She hadn't said goodbye to her past; she'd been bound to it again.

***

Early the next morning the wintry frost coated the windows of the house and van. Hope had carefully packed and prepared the passenger van throughout the cold night before. Hope sat in the Ethereal and beige patterned armchair, rubbing the sharp pain spiraling down her spine with spiced oil extracts and a grey-ish cotton cloth. She had long stopped trying to explain her pain to anyone—especially Jim. Decades of trauma had carved it into her body like a second skeleton. She told herself it was just the cost of motherhood, a result of the last two C-sections and endless lifting and bending. But the truth lay buried deeper, beneath an illegal gag order issued by a family court judge who, at the time, was still a judge, and is now in private practice with an impeccable record. Hope's body knew what it knew. The reflexes she once used to shield her children from Corbin's wrath were the same ones that made her a natural at martial arts. She had taught Emma, Leo, and Sebastian every block and roll she could remember—not just for play, but for something more that she couldn't quite recall—until they grew taller and better than her. She still played with Sebastian, Anna and the twins, usually only after a pain procedure when her inflamed nerves were temporarily silenced by medically deafened synapses. Her mind drifted to the not-so- distant past.

She'd been scheduled for a procedure in the morning. Jim knew that. Marsi, their teenage babysitter, was going to drive her there and back while Emma, Leo, and Sebastian helped their younger siblings, and Jim stayed behind to work in his adjacent shop.

Jim had appeared in the doorway the night before, in suit and tie instead, the temple recommend peeking from his pocket like a badge, the sharp light he kept in the hallway infusing the bedroom, where she lay exhausted; the children far past asleep, too.

"They scheduled bishopric interviews for tonight. You need to be present."

"Jim, the hospital—my spine—the ablations are in the morning, you remember, right?"

"Pain is temporary, Hope. Covenants are eternal."

His rebuff was firm as he handed her a walker with that same detached calm, then took her phone from her hand, dialed the surgeon on call, and rescheduled without asking—her permission was non-requisite.

"They may have a cancellation next month," he said. "You'll need to call to confirm in the morning. See? It worked out. Let's go. You've made us late."

Hope said nothing. Her scalp already tingled, anticipating the oil on her head, the circle of hands, the performance.

She shuddered at the memory and pulled herself up to finish packing the van, ensuring that every last document and every precious person with their own personal cargo made it.

Her pain—real and daily—was not holy enough for this house.

***

At 15 years old, just one year younger than his older sister Ella, Leo sat quietly beside his siblings' packed bags, his hands folded too neatly in his lap, wrapped in thick gloves, a thick black knit snow hat partially covering his dappled soft wheat hair, a similar black scarf around his thick neck, billows of silver air cascading through his lightly parted lips as it mixed with the sharp and frigid winter's sting. Hope caught the way his jaw tightened, his somber eyes flickering with a mixture of sorrow and resolve that seemed far too grown for someone still clinging to childhood.

He's carrying more than he should, she thought. Trying to be the man his father never was.

But Leo wasn't just thinking about the next few hours—he was thinking years ahead. In his mind, he pictured himself standing in front of a podium, tall and certain, recounting the truths that no one else had dared to say aloud. He would name names, tell the world who Jim really was behind closed doors. He would expose the coldness, the silence, the long stares of disdain passed off as discipline, and other things. Someday, when he had the power, when he had his own voice and wasn't just one of "her kids," he'd make sure the world knew what happened in that house. He wasn't afraid to remember. And he'd ensure no one else forgot. He watched his mother limp; and wanted to help her, but couldn't seem to make himself move. Frozen like the trees surrounding them, Leo felt like time was moving too slow and too fast all at once.

Hope wanted to reach for him, to say something that might ease the invisible burdens he bore—but the words wouldn't come. Not now. She hadn't been able to pierce through his exterior before. This was not the time or place. Not with Sammy squirming in her arms and the road ahead pressing in with a weight that made her chest ache. She handed Sammy to Anna, and bade her back inside with the twins for warmer outerwear and base layers inside their pillowcases, as Emma and Sebastian circled in helping to ice off the windows.

Hope turned to the next task in the bright morning sun reflecting off the blindingly icy frosted terrain.

She had asked each of the children to pack what mattered most: three sets of clothes, one favorite item, their pillow, and their journals. Once the van was loaded with their belongings, she checked on her work from the night before—all was intact— the legal boxes; re-filed them by court date, and the last bin held voice recordings—court-mandated calls, therapy notes, medical files.

She didn't have power. But she had proof.

"No one forgets this," she'd whispered, closing the last of the file boxes.

The bins of records were under the bench seat. Inside them wasn't just documentation—it was a trail of memory. Voice recordings from court-supervised calls. Medical records with words like *"injury consistent with blunt force trauma."* Not one of them had ever been enough to stop Corbin. But if someday any of her children doubted what had happened, doubted her, the proof would still be there. Not for vengeance, but for truth.

She checked the gas tank, taped an emergency phone list to the glove box, and tucked the kids' birth certificates under the seat.

It wasn't everything. But it was enough.

Everyone grabbed a seat. Leo called shotgun-navigator for the first stretch.

Hope buckled Sammy into his car seat, each motion mechanical and deliberate—because if she stopped to feel, she might not keep moving. Then she drove, steering them far from everything they'd known, toward the slim hope of safety.

***

Each day she drove further. She asked. Every shelter she reached was just as she'd feared—already packed beyond capacity. But what she hadn't anticipated—and what gutted her most—was the policy that every shelter she came across upheld:

"We don't accept boys over twelve years old. Sorry. They would be—er, triggers."

Astonishment turned to horror, then to fury. What of Sebastian? What of Leo? How could these gentle, thoughtful boys—barely into adolescence—be seen as threats, unfit for refuge?

The realization struck Hope like a thunderclap: the system that claimed to protect was built with cracks wide enough to lose her children through. This wasn't just a matter of space; it was a matter of being erased by bureaucracy, cast aside by policies that made no space for teenage boys fleeing with their mothers.

"Now what?!" she whispered to herself, gripping the wheel until her knuckles whitened. "What of my kind, brilliant Sebastian? My strong, protective Leo?"

Hope drove on in silence, her mind racing with possibilities and contingency plans. Emma, Leo and Sebastian took turns in the front to stretch their legs and learned to navigate maps. She headed south for Rhode

Island, toward the Gideons' and her Father's haven—and what she still dared to hope might be a true home. But even as she drove, her thoughts carried her further still, toward an uncertain horizon where justice and safety remained heartbreakingly out of reach. So she turned the wheel and kept driving— further south, toward something like freedom.

***

Author's Note

Hope's journey is not just a personal tragedy—it is an indictment of systemic failure. From the overt brutality of Corbin's sadistic abuse to the covert, soul- eroding neglect and psychological manipulation by Jim, we witness how both grandiose and subtle forms of control can dismantle identity, shatter families, and endanger generations. These abuses— physical, emotional, spiritual—flourish under the guise of love, religiosity, and the law when left unchecked.

This story also lays bare the dangerous influence of institutions—especially those that conflate religious control with divine authority. The rebranding of "Mormonism" as the "Church of Jesus Christ of Latter-day Saints" is more than a marketing shift; it represents a deeper identity heist, one that risks misleading vulnerable seekers into harmful theological and doctrinal traps disguised as truth. When churches or legal systems protect abusers or prioritize power over protection, they do not merely fail—they participate in the erasure of the human soul.

Ask yourself: If you were Hope—or her friend, parent, or pastor—what would you do? What should churches, communities, and courts be doing now to intervene for mothers and their children still caught in these cycles? No structure, no title, and no tradition is above question when it becomes a tool of destruction.

Every quiet act of defiance, every whisper of truth, and every survivor who speaks is a living testament that control can be challenged—and the human spirit, no matter how battered, still fights to rise.

Chapter 11

Race to Times Past Forward: Last Winter - Yesterday Morning

Hope's battered hands trembled as she dialed yet another shelter hotline—a familiar ritual by now. On the long, winding road from Maine back to Rhode Island, she had spoken with four domestic violence shelters, only to be gently turned away. Each receptionist's sympathetic tone faded quickly when the screening revealed two boys over twelve—deemed "triggers" too volatile for their safe havens. Each call ended with the same sorrowful news: there was no vacancy, no space for her family today; not with boys over twelve years old. The receptionist's soft, apologetic tone felt as cold and final as a locked door, yet Hope clung to the promise that safety would be found elsewhere.

With each call serving as a painful reminder of the barriers still in place, Hope knew that her only option for the time being was the temporary lodging arranged by a charitable organization. From early December through mid-January, a charity funded by a Domestic Violence Organization provided lodging for her family at a rundown motel.

Inside, the air was thick with ceaseless noise: constant chatter from those awake from 11 at night until 4 in the morning, and a pervasive silence by day—punctuated only by the muffled sounds of abuse echoing from the adjoining rooms. A bullet, lodged stubbornly in a wall near a row of grimy windows, served as an unyielding reminder of a violent past. Cigarette butts, carelessly strewn along the windowsill, mocked any semblance of order. Hope's heart pounded as she realized that in this transient refuge, the only thing left untouched was the bullet—a symbol of violence too raw to erase. She could not remove the bullet from the wall, fix the sagging floor, mend the tattered blinds, or patch the frayed, no-longer-white thin bed covers.

***

Leo moaned to his older sister, Emma, "Why are we here? We didn't do anything wrong. It seems like the only people who can help us won't, Em. Just because they don't want to and are afraid to get involved themselves. If we ever get home, why should I help any of them when they fall on hard times? Emma, Mom says so often that this is not our home; that Christ is our prize, and eternity there must be more unimaginable than anything on earth. I just want all of that—now, Em. I'm just so tired; does that make sense?"

Emma urged, "Leo, don't talk like that! You can't give up! I need you. Mom needs us both, and we're a family. Isn't that what matters? Don't you remember what Mom says... 'There is no way out, just through?' Leo, I need you; we all do, because with you, we can go through anything. But only if we go through it together, all right? I can't do this without you!"

Leo looked up at Emma, his grey-green eyes glistening with tears. "Why didn't Dad ever call us, Em? Not even—Thanksgiving? Christmas?"

Emma swept her younger brother into her arms and whispered defiantly into his ear, "Who is your father, Leo? The man in the castle we left, or the One who created and chose you because He knew you would choose Him back one day? Remember who you are, in Christ, brother. Straighten your non- Mormon crown. Your Father is calling, through our Brother, our Savior, our Lord. Are you going to answer?"

Leo grabbed his sister's neck and sobbed, "Pray with me, Em? I need to hear His voice..." as his sister huddled beside him, and together they cried out to their Savior and Father in muffled words intended for privacy in a crowded room.

***

There was a faint knock at the entry door, and Hope left the chain locked as she clasped the flimsy brass knob to open the door a crack.

"Can I help you?" Hope's voice turned to the weeping woman in the hallway, who had a little boy, about 6 or 7 years old, petting a large black standard poodle that was shrieking.

The woman before her appeared to be another mother—her eyes red and determined, clutching her autistic son's medical service dog's leash. This woman's son, with special needs and a lifeline in the form of that highly trained and devoted canine, was being forced to return with his mother to their abuser because the shelter refused to accommodate the dog despite its training and the boy's needs.

"I am so sorry! That's just awful!" Hope nearly wept with her. "What can I do?" she repeated, stammering.

"Nothing," the woman sobbed. "I just thought I saw you praying another day, and you seemed kind with your children, so…"

"Oh my, of course! Would you like to pray together?" Hope asked as the battered, broken woman nodded. Hope slipped the chain open, turning her back to the door and asking Sebastian to watch Sammy for a moment, holding the thin brown door slightly open behind her as she met her likeness in the dingy hallway.

"Would you? I…I'm out of words," the mother wept.

"Lord Jesus, in Your Sacred Name and Holy Blood do we dare boldly approach the throne of grace of The Father Who sent You. Father, we ask, through the Holy Spirit that binds us, for Your presence. We need miracles, breakthroughs, mountains moved that we cannot move on our own. Thank You for being our God who hears, for putting those in power who hear and act on our behalf to win the battles beyond our strength alone. You say that we are Your children and that You care for Your flock, but our eyes are weary and strained. We don't know what to do or where to go, but we fix our gaze on You alone. The cross before us, the world behind us, no turning back. We don't know what to do, Lord, but where else do we turn but to You? In our Savior's Holy Sacred name, we pray and seek Your help. Amen."

Hope fumbled as the mother before her, named Violet, nodded, and they hugged in the hallway laden with no-smoking signs yet filled with cigarette and vape smoke.

Hope slipped back into the small room as Violet led her son and service dog down the stairwell back to the batterer she had fled from.

As Hope closed the door behind Violet, the weight of their shared desperation settled like dust in the stagnant air. Around her, the motel's walls seemed to close in tighter, whispering of the many families trapped within its crumbling embrace.

***

Hope and her seven children learned the harsh rhythm of life in that motel: the cacophony of voices that never truly quieted, the taste of stale air mixed with bitter memories, and the ever-present reminder of the bullet lodged in a cracked wall, where it had barely missed an infant's head. There were roach baits placed around the floor of the room, and cigarette butts scattered like ghostly confetti along the windowsill that they had all seen their mother try to sweep away before they noticed. The old motel, with its dim, smoke-filled corridors and peeling layers of paint, was a temporary refuge—far from a sanctuary, yet shelter enough against the storms in houses, not homes, and the bitter cold outside or the blazing heat of homelessness.

Each night, Hope lay on a thin, creaking cot in a room that smelled of must. She listened to the muted sobs and hushed whispers of others sharing similar fates, knowing her children heard it too. In those moments, the pain of rejection mingled with the sharp pains through her spine and the tang of cold metal and unsanitary fabric. It was a brutal reminder that safety was still just beyond reach.

Hope's phone vibrated. Dad's House (Church Line) flashed onscreen—a number she hadn't dialed in years. "Remember the cedar chest. Spare key where the roses were." The words were code for a truth she scarcely believed: her father's donated home now served as a safe house under the church's benevolent arm. She thumb-typed back with trembling hands: "Children need sanctuary. ETA unknown. Please keep the gate unlocked."

The reply came swiftly, "No names; no promises. Only some hope," the words soon distilled to pixels.

A new bubble popped up from Jim, requesting her consent to an immediate divorce:

"You've abandoned me...It doesn't matter anyway. As a man, I can be Sealed to as many women as I want. You remember her, don't you, Hope? Sister Darringer? Marsi from up the street was the children's babysitter whenever you were in the hospital (delivering another baby) from our church Ward; not that you'd care now if you aren't even attending any longer. You may have your children now, but mind your eternal consequences, Hope, at least for the children, or I will have to mind them on your behalf."

Her thumb went numb; the screen blurred. Somewhere behind her, Leo whispered a Psalm to steady himself. The motel's air conditioner kicked on, exhaling a breath colder than the text.

The chill of more than thirty years lost to the men Hope could not leave without Eternal Damnation, but who could have as many Eternal wives, including her, in the Afterlife, seeped into every crevice holding Hope together. Corbin had already remarried and divorced three women, each with multiple children, in search of his next window-dressing wife, while ever-growing Jemma and Fowley were just along for his show and tell. Suddenly, a woman's voice cackled in her ear—a voice from several lifetimes ago, one that, like Corbin's or Jim's, would forever wrench Hope to the core. "Hehehe, Hope! You expecting FAIR?!" WHACK! "Life!" WHACK! "ISN'T!" WHACK! "FAIR!" WHACK! And whizzzzz went her steel- tipped wig brush through the air, landing wherever it happened to upon Hope's clearly lacking and foolish body, if she needed to be taught with such force.

Years past tears, Hope thought, "Wow, I forgot that lesson. You were right. Life's not fair, is it? No matter how I try to be." Hope's mind wandered. "Even the tiniest spark of light erases darkness, though," the thought trailed through, alongside others similar.

That night, as she lay awake while her children slept outside the Dindy Motel door, a diesel engine idled—too clean, too deliberate for this neighborhood. Headlights swept the blinds, slicing bars of blinding white across the peeling wallpaper. Hope's heart hammered. "Please let it be Amy and Paul"—then the engine faded, leaving behind only the low electric hum of the coming dawn. She exhaled: deliverance was on the road, not yet at the door. A second thought caught her breath as her heart skipped a beat.

"Had that been someone sent by Jim or Corbin to find us?"

Hypervigilance is healthy when warranted—altogether a different slice of pie than paranoia.

***

Suddenly, on January 14th, as if a long-awaited sigh of relief, the family's fortunes shifted—they were transferred from the chaos of the motel to the quiet sanctuary of a promised Safe House that Hope had not dared to dream of.

The family was moved to a farmhouse—a Safe House reminiscent of the only home Hope had ever known at her father's. The farmhouse, nestled in a sprawling, dew-drenched field bordered by rustling cornstalks and weathered barns, exuded a quiet, steadfast warmth. The wood-paneled walls creaked softly with age, and the windows framed expansive views of sun- dappled pastures.

A large stone fireplace in the living room offered the comforting, steady glow of embers, and the faint aroma of freshly baked bread and simmering stew danced through the air, as if it were her father's home, welcoming her youngest children this time. It was a haven that whispered of both refuge and renewal—a stark contrast to the despair of the dismal motel that kept the family together and out of Foster Care; being homeless with children is illegal and grounds for their removal from custody to be placed in the well-funded Foster Care System.

But even here, as the farmhouse began to mend the family's frayed edges, a new and daunting reality loomed: Hope had to find work—and fast. After decades of outwardly enforced unemployment due to the crippling effects of abuse, her body bore irreparable scars that made every movement an agonizing trial, yet the weight of rent and bills pressed upon her relentlessly.

With the farmhouse now their temporary home, Hope resolved to search for employment, despite her disabilities and the physical and mental toll it would require of her and impact each of her children. The thought alone sent shivers from her head through her tailbone—her aging, trembling fingers brushed over a faded job posting pamphlet in the quiet morning light filtering through lace curtains.

***

As she homeschooled her seven children, Hope also began filling out job applications. No one had ever told her that she qualified for Disability Benefits—despite her crippling pain, her inability to sit for long stretches, her impaired hand-eye coordination from a traumatic brain injury, and the long work history she had built from the age of fifteen until her body simply could not endure anymore.

Hope had to begin immediately to pay rent, provide the needed food and clothing for her growing children, and cover gas and car repairs for the employment she must find right away in order to comply with the Safe House's regulations—or risk eviction. She had to work, somehow, after an entire married life where her labor had been confined to the invisible world of homeschooling and survival, as she and Jim had once agreed.

Late at night, after exhausting hours of job hunting on an old, sputtering computer, cooking, cleaning, tending to her little ones' needs, and homeschooling, Hope would retreat to a corner of the farmhouse's sparse kitchen. There, with only the soft glow of a single bulb overhead, she unfurled a thick stack of weathered legal transcripts and scraps of medical records that stretched back twenty-one years.

In those quiet hours, Hope's mind—sharpened by years of survival and innate tenacity—began to piece together the sources of her many injuries. She discovered the roots of the pain that had haunted her body: why she had choked so often on food; why her neck throbbed with every movement; why her legs sometimes refused to bear her weight. A long-postponed neck surgery, she realized with bittersweet hope, might yet save some of what remained. At least they could replace two of her four eroded discs. No fusions yet. Some part of her was still intact.

Page after page revealed what Hope had never been allowed to name: her memories had not merely faded over time. They had been systematically normalized, minimized, and silenced—by those she trusted, by the systems meant to protect her, by a court that sealed away the truth with a Gag Order issued in secret.

The crisp rustle of paper, the antiseptic smell lingering on old medical reports, the relentless ticking of the farmhouse clock—these became a symphony of revelation. Her mind, conditioned to endure agony in silence, began to awaken. Every bruised rib, every compressed disc, every scar mapped the violence she had suffered at the hands of Corbin, her so-called protector, her so-called priesthood leader. Violence often inflicted while her children slept—or even while they watched.

"Blame on them and shame OFF me," her father's pastor had once said, and the words sliced through the infection of lies she had carried for too long.

Her body might have been broken, but it bore the witnesses of truth, now sharp within her mind and freshly awakened memories. Her legal and medical journals and those of the Mormon/Latter-Day-Saint Organization, hidden in her father's hearth, were like a map, pointing the way forward— not only for her own survival but for her children and their children.

Hope's youngest children, even now, were learning to "forget what happened on purpose"—the same survival tactic that had almost destroyed her. If the cycle was to end, they would need to confront the truth, not bury it.

Hope was determined that her children would not become easy targets for the next generation of predators—whether Jemma, Fowley, Jim, or Corbin. For memory, painful though it was, would be their armor. And forgetting, however tempting, would only ensure they became victims again.

***

As the first light of a pale morning crept over the farmhouse, Hope gathered her seven children into the snug living room. The scent of apple breakfast cake, slow-baking in the old oven, wrapped around them like a fragile promise of warmth.

There, amid the soft murmurs of a family slowly beginning to heal, Hope spoke—with a voice both resolute and raw.

"Are we family?" she whispered, her words deliberate, designed to ignite their full attention.

The children stared at her, dazed, exchanging glances as if asking each other silently:

Of course, we are. Why is she asking? What does she mean?

Then, in a chorus of shy nods and murmured affirmations, they answered: "Yes."

Hope pressed on, her voice steady.

"Then your last names are not just Richardson," she said, her eyes sweeping the room. "They are also Livingston—my father's name, the name tied to the Bible he lived by and the church he loved."

She continued, drawing each child closer with her soft spoken, slow and purposeful words.

"Each of us, including me, has a past we cannot afford to erase. No matter how much anyone tries to steal it from us or convince us to forget—even the painful memories, even the joyful ones that hard times try to bury—we must remember. Especially the memories that shaped us into who we are."

Hope paused, then spoke even more quietly, as though weaving truth into their shattered souls and tattered spirits.

"We must use our past from this day forward. To learn from it together. To remind each other so that we don't fall again without understanding why—and so that when we do fall, we know how to rise differently. Do you understand?"

Some of the younger children looked puzzled, so Hope turned to the older ones: "Emma, Leo, Sebastian... what do you hear in what I just said?"

After a long silence, Leo answered quietly.

"I think you're saying we have to face our past. All of it—the anger, the hurt... even when it burns. If we don't, we'll stay trapped in the same cycle. Dad's anger. Fowley's cruelty. Jemma's lies. It's all part of us now. If we don't become something different... we'll become just like them."

He hesitated, then finished, his voice trembling with conviction.

"But we have each other. We lift each other up when we fall. Is this it, Mom?" The words hung between them like a solemn promise—and a challenge.

Outside, the farmhouse stood as a quiet sentinel against a world still steeped in cruelty—a small beacon of awakening light, defying the relentless cold of the past and the pressures of the present. Hope nodded to Leo, tears burning behind her eyes. She watched as each child, in their own words and ways, built upon his insight. Their mother listened, encouraged, and gently urged them on or let it lay, weaving a tapestry of shared truth among them, and opened doors for their truths to unfold as a family.

Long-hidden abscesses of grief and betrayal broke open, not to destroy them, but to heal.

Each lie exposed to the light made space for a new truth to be planted, like seeds sown into once-wounded soil. In their raw and unvarnished voices, Hope heard the first tentative budding of new life—fragile, but real.

The farmhouse itself seemed to hold them gently, like a hand-stitched quilt against the cold: a sanctuary not just of shelter, but of truth.

Hope's seven youngest children, who had never before seen their mother's childhood fields in Rhode Island, now sat surrounded by them—finally close enough to remember, and perhaps, to belong.

In the kitchen, as the apple cake neared completion, Hope scrambled eggs and sliced fruit. She called her children to the large farmhouse table for breakfast before their schoolwork began—and before she herself would return to her desperate search for work.

Hope's journey had become a race against time: a fight not only to survive but to reclaim the very pieces of herself that had been stolen, erased, or beaten down over decades.

She knew what was at stake.

If her children allowed themselves to forget, as she had once been taught to forget, the darkness that had swallowed her would consume them too.

But if they remembered—if they carried the truth forward—they could break the cycle. They could build a future no longer chained to the crimes of the past.

And that morning, in the quiet hum of a battered but healing farmhouse, Hope vowed that they would do just that.

***

Author's Note:

A lot can happen in a short time. Ironically, the catalyst that "woke Hope up" to the reasons for her injuries, the causes of her debilitating pain and hidden traumas, and her lost life was the threat of death to her youngest children by those whom the courts repeatedly ushered back into Corbin's sole custody for repeated injuries. Until that moment, Jemma and Fowley were as much Hope's children in her heart and mind as her youngest ones, and those who had died at birth during her marriage to Corbin.

It wasn't until Hope forced herself to wade back through the boxes of her own legal and medical trauma in an attempt to find a future for her children that she was compelled to read her own words and piece together the shards of herself that had been shattered by Corbin's legal and monstrous misuse— misuse that is as commonplace as any weapon in the wrong hands today. While searching through terminology, she encountered two phrases that, as the humble author, I do not know where to place in this account of her life except here: Adult Child Alienation Syndrome; a form of child abuse not yet recognized by Family Courts; a tactic often associated with "Father's Rights" groups and a handbook written by Dick Hart titled, "*Screw the Bitch,*" which has been in print and available online for decades. The phenomenon of Child Alienation vs. natural Child Estrangement mirrors Jemma and Fowley's characters in that both exhibit strong negative emotions toward their protective parent, Hope, as expressed by their perpetrator(s), perhaps with a portion of their own feelings or experiences inflamed and exaggerated to resemble the perpetrator or abusive parent's thoughts—not a factual account of the relationship with the non-offending and protective parent. The difference between child alienation and child estrangement is vast. Rightful estrangement in children like Jemma and Fowley occurred when they were young and had not seen Corbin for some time; it was natural for Jemma, who had been both directly physically and mentally harmed by Corbin and indirectly victimized by being forced to experience her father's physical and psychological abuse against both her mother and brother. Child estrangement is a child naturally pulling away from an abusive parent. Child alienation is a forced wedge of hate inflicted upon a child toward a victimized parent by the perpetrator of abuse. Typically, adults who have experienced child alienation exhibit emotions rooted and shaped by the perpetrator, often with one or several incidents exaggerated in the adult child's mind, seeded and watered by the child's primary abuser: it isn't safe to get upset with the abusive parent, even as an adult, when the child has experienced high levels of trauma, right?

See Lundy Bancroft; *Why Does He Do That? Inside the Minds of Angry and Controlling Men*, 1st Edition

and www.batteredmotherscustodyconference.com - For Help

According to Psychology Today in 2024, when Hope was researching,

"there are three times as many children in the United States who are alienated from a parent than there are children with autism."

https://www.psychologytoday.com/us/blog/head-games/202112/the- devastating-effects-of-parental-alienation

For more detailed accounts of this small but significant chapter, please read the companion book,

Divine Theft: How a Rebranded Faith Is Fueling a Political Coup and Threatening Our Future by Lindsay McGuire; for a full expansion of this chapter, a deeper dive into Hope's youngest children's characters, and their discoveries throughout this timeline.

Epilogue:
Present Day

R ain weeps across the farmhouse roof in relentless sheets, drumming a dirge on warped shingles. Lightning spiderwebs the sky, carving bone-white veins into the night. Inside, every room sits hush-dim—

furniture shrouded in linen, memories cloaked in grief. Emma stands by the front window, her forehead pressed to the cold glass, watching rainwater braid down the pane like tears she refuses to shed.

Somewhere beyond the oak door, heavy footsteps squelch in the mud—deliberate, unhurried. Each thud echoes the unanswered questions she carries like stones.

Hope's seven children gather around their mother's lifeless body, mourning and comforting one another, wondering aloud what comes next. Tears spill from their splotched red cheeks as they embrace, clinging to one another while Emma and Leo remain unmoving—steadfast, like the mother who raised them.

As the sun glows bright and begins to dim on the horizon in dapples of red, purple, and rose-hued light, a different tune by Maverick City Music flows faintly through the living room—about being free. Hope's oldest daughter gently asks each sibling to share what they love most about their Momma and what they look forward to most about seeing her again in Heaven.

Together, the children place their tiniest to mid-sized hands on their mother's—her hands, her arms, her heart. They clasp each other's hands in turn, praising, praying, aching. Emma speaks first, brimming with tears she will not shed in front of them. She saves those for when she is alone.

At sixteen, Emma is resolute. She will carry on her mother's legacy and fight to keep their family together.

She is painfully aware that at thirteen and fifteen, Sebastian and Leo are too old for most domestic violence shelters. No matter how gentle, kind, or traumatized they are, boys above twelve are seen as "triggers" to the other mothers—an unspoken, heartbreaking bias, despite anti-discrimination policies.

She also knows her battle extends beyond shelter rules. Ten-year-old Anna, eight-year-old twins Molly and Matthew, and little Sammy each face uncertain futures. And Emma, though wise beyond her years, is still just sixteen—legally too young to gain custody. Even though she has graduated early, been accepted into college for the fall, and stayed local for them, none of it guarantees their family will remain whole.

Rain clouds gather again. A distant thundercrack rolls in. Raindrops tap the roof and rattle the windowpanes—like shared tears grieving with Hope's youngest, in place of the emotions the eldest refuses to show.

On the mantel rests a shard of stained glass from the Safe House window—red on opalescent, the color scheme Hope always said represented courage bleeding into purity. Emma fingers the edge until a bead of blood surfaces. A fitting covenant, she thinks: a little red to keep the white honest.

Thunder rolls. Footsteps mount the porch—one... two... three—then pause at the threshold. Floorboards groan like weary prayers. The children freeze, breaths halved, memories of pipe-bomb threats lingering like smoke. Then silence. Only rain and the slow crack-pop of the cooling stove. The past, it seems, knows every road here—yet chooses, for now, to circle rather than knock.

Emma steels herself. *I've passed my SATs. I can work and go to college part-time... Leo can get a job too. Mom's insurance might be enough to buy a house like this. But will that money even come to me? Am I old enough? Or will Dad?*

Her thoughts spin. *Will we be sent back to him? To Jim? To his new wife and that cruel babysitter, Marsi? Will he file just to claim us for the taxes and let Jemma and Fowley erase our lives like they promised—and nearly did those years ago? He's proven, in action and through words, that were harder than any rock or stick he could have hurled at me, at Mom, at all of us—that he cares more about them than us. He never believed me. Never took my side. Any of our sides! He says WE are the mistakes! Well, Jemma and Fowley, they're not even his! HE'S the mistake!"* Emma's thoughts spiraled, leaving no trace on her face.

Inside, Emma's vibrant spirit was fracturing, shattered by the terroristic bomb threats made against her and her minor siblings—felonies that their mother could get no DA or prosecutor in any state to prosecute. Blessings to the perpetrators, Jemma and Fowley, again Scott free. Again, their splattered victims bear the consequences of what they've just walked away from. Torturous crimes that no child, no mother, no family should be forced to face or defend themselves against.

Across the room, Sebastian clenches his fists—grief, betrayal, and terror transforming into silent fury. His thoughts race. *Maybe it's worse if we're separated... sent to foster care. What if I can't protect them?*

An electric bolt of hope flashes through him. *Maybe someone at the new Christian church will help. Or Grandpa's old one. Could it be like those early Christians who rescued those whom Rome threw away? Or is this just another false version of faith—like the Mormonism we fled?*

His thirteen-year-old heart flounders in helpless desperation as the music swells, the lyrics about freedom clashing with the suffocating fear inside him.

Suddenly, footsteps pound on the wet front porch. A stairboard creaks beneath heavy weight.

Emma motions for everyone to stay still. Quiet. But Leo moves toward the cellar door.

Who is it? their minds scream. *Have Fowley and Jemma found the Safe Home? Is it their dad? His babysitter wife? A social worker here to take them away?*

A heavy knock shudders the farmhouse door. Rain surges louder. Thunder cracks.

And time holds its breath.

Words From the Author

"I am only one, but still I am one. I cannot do everything, but still I can do something; and because I cannot do everything, I will not refuse to do something that I can do." - Helen Keller

As Hope's story in this life ends, her children's story is only just beginning— and with it, a rallying cry is birthed, passing the torch to you. Their voices remind us that our systems must change to protect those who cannot protect themselves.

Nearly one in three women—and countless children of both genders— experience war crimes and abuses as Hope and her children did every day.

This staggering reality demands urgent action.

Accountability and reform are not optional; they are moral and humanitarian imperatives.

As you turn through these final pages filled with resources that only your voice can uniquely witness, the clock is still ticking. Their story—and the story of countless others—is not yet over.

Ask yourself:

Are you still sitting on the sidelines? If so, why? What will your legacy be?

Your silence speaks as loudly as any whisper. How will you choose to be moved by this achingly true story?

Will you help end the cycles of abuse and inhumane injustice, or will you be one who walks away, intentionally dismissive of all you've encountered within these pages?

Will you cry out for the enactment of Coercive Control and Abusive Litigation Laws now, before another human life suffers a fate like that of Hope and her children? Or will your silence become your legacy after the revolution?

Will you demand mandatory education for judges, law enforcement, prosecutors, and district attorneys—to protect the vulnerable rather than betray them? Or are you more influenced by the perpetrators among us? What will your stance say about you?

If you partner with organizations like <u>Alliance for Hope International</u>, leaders in strangulation prevention, family justice models, and recovery camps for traumatized youth, do you realize how desperately your voice is needed to silence the intentionally deafened ears and hardened hearts of those with too much power and little, if any, accountability?

Maybe, just maybe, a bold few will rise to strip away the disguises of powerful institutions that hoard billions under false religious exemptions while families like Hope's suffer in silence.

If Hope's voice has stirred something in you, **please—be the change**. For Hope's children. For Hope.

For every survivor still waiting to be heard. Her journals whisper even now:

"Hope doesn't stop—it cannot afford to. Neither can you."

Your voice matters. Your courage matters.

Your actions will save lives.

It has been my deepest honor to tell Hope's story, woven from her journals, her notes, and the memories of those who loved her most.

If this book has moved you, please purchase them as gifts; bulk discounts available; with donations from each book and audiobook purchase supporting initiatives to sustain families like Hope's.

This book series is more than a tribute.

It is a call for overdue systemic reforms.

If you hear that call—**answer it**: Together, we can shape a future where no child's identity is stolen, and no survivor's suffering is silenced.

—Lindsay McGuire

Afterword: Resources for Support and Action

T his section provides practical tools and trusted resources for those seeking support or looking to drive change in the fight against domestic abuse and systemic injustice. *(All information was verified*

as publicly available at the time of publication. Please consult the official websites or local offices for the most current details.)

Domestic Violence Support National Domestic Violence Hotline
Phone: 1-800-799-7233

Website: www.thehotline.org

Available 24/7 to provide confidential support and crisis intervention. Typically calls are outsourced to local levels reached just by calling 211 in your area. Check your United Way.

National Coalition Against Domestic Violence (NCADV)
Website: www.ncadv.org

Offers statistical data and resources for professionals and funds **THL HOTLINE** above.

Futures Without Violence

Phone: (202) 296-4141

Website: www.futureswithoutviolence.org

Provides tools for survivors, prevention programs, and policy advocacy.

RAINN (Rape, Abuse & Incest National Network)
Phone: 1-800-656-4673

Website: hotline.rainn.org/online

Operates the National Sexual Assault Hotline and provides support for survivors of sexual violence. Excellent resource for victims needing actionable help.

Legal Support and Advocacy Women's Law
Website: www.womenslaw.org

Legal information and state-specific guidance for women experiencing abuse, including help with custody, restraining orders, and court proceedings. Helping victims for over 25 years.

Legal Services Corporation (LSC)
Website: www.lsc.gov

Directory of nonprofit legal aid providers serving low-income and vulnerable individuals, including survivors of abuse.

National Domestic Violence Legal Hotline

Website: www.ndvlh.org

Provides legal advice, referrals, and help navigating the court system.

Legal Momentum

Website: www.legalmomentum.org

Advocates for the legal rights of women and girls through litigation and policy initiatives.

Find and Contact Government Officials:

- *U.S. Congress and Senate Contact Info:*www.congress.gov | www.usa.gov/elected-officials
- *White House Contact Page:*www.whitehouse.gov/contact
- *National Conference of State Legislatures:*www.ncsl.org
- *GovTrack – Find Your Representatives:*www.govtrack.us

To locate your own state legislature, search "[Your State] Legislature" or "[Your State] Governor's Office" online for accurate directories and contact information.

Advocacy Tip: Craft personalized letters or emails using information from official sites. Template campaigns are also available on platforms like Change.org and MoveOn.organd in the *Identity Heist* companion books and workbooks.

Understanding Abuse Cycles and Coercive Control

MindBodyGreen

Website: www.mindbodygreen.com

Covers trauma-related responses such as fight, flight, freeze, and fawn.

Verywell Mind – Complex PTSD

Website: www.verywellmind.com

Explains symptoms, recovery strategies, and expert-backed research on long- term trauma.

International Labour Organization – Modern Slavery and Lxploitation

Website: www.ilo.org

Resources and reports on global exploitation, including domestic servitude.

How You Can Help

If this book has inspired you to take action:

- Share this book to purchase with others to spread awareness.
- Check out the Identity Heist Companion books to buy, read, apply, and recommend.
- Begin the **#movehopeforward** initiative
- Reach out to someone who may need help, and offer these resources.
- Support or volunteer with organizations working to end abuse.
- Contact your legislators to advocate for stronger protections for victim/ survivors, and persist with the #movehopeforward iiinitiative.

Every effort matters. Change begins with awareness and is carried forward through collective courage and action.

*More awareness and advocacy guides are found in the Identity Heist Workbook Companion Guide(s). Bulk discounts available. A portion of every Lindsay McGuire book sale financially supports victim/survivor resources.

Acknowledgments

To my **Ama**, whose soft whisper in the dark taught me that a voice could be a pen—and later, a word.

    To my Pappa, whose steady hands and pure heart showed me that strength is born of love, even when the ground quakes. Without you both— my first protectors, my parents—this story would not exist. I owe you every single word.

To my family, who stood in the wreckage with me—your cheers and prayers became my armor, your laughter my lifeline, and the spark that urged me to share Hope's story. You believed in these pages long before I dared to write them. Thank you for your faith, endurance, and boundless love.

To Jonathon Kendall, my Preface author: Your world-class wisdom and seven-figure successes have never overshadowed the generosity of your time with me and Hope. Thank you for reading these pages with more than just a mentor's open heart and for crafting a preface so meticulously that it feels like wings beneath my words. Your humility cloaks a brilliance that now elevates Hope's story to heights I could never have imagined. That gift— your voice, your insight, your belief—lifts this work beyond anything I dared to dream. I am forever grateful for your guidance and this brilliantly articulated introduction.

To my Lditors-in-Chief, Perry and Yasmine: Your radiant optimism and masterful edits have birthed this work and Hope's very first books into being. You've helped me create more than just a book; you've ushered in volumes inspired by Hope and others yet to come. May your beautiful spirits resonate with every page turn, and may the blessings you lavish so freely return to you a thousand-fold.

To the real-life Hope and your children: My heart breaks alongside yours for every layer of loss and injury you have endured. May this book—and those that follow—bring purpose to your pain, honor your journey, and uplift all who bear similar scars and secrets. May my fumbling, imperfect sentences carry your memory forward, Hope. You have captured my heart and compelled me to do anything for you and those you loved.

Words fall short of my love, gratitude, and prayers for each of you.

To my co-author: my forever breath, my Savior, and my Lord, the risen Messiah and the Biblical God: Thank You for showing me that Yours is the only 'wild love' that makes mankind whole. Your identity is joyfully forever beyond capture or containment. Thank You for Your life in me—without You, I am nothing, but in Your presence?!?! I pray this work is right in Your sight and return it to You, trusting You to correct it in the heart and mind of each reader or listener. Love undefined—from Your broken vessel back to You.

—Lindsay McGuire

About The Author

Lindsay McGuire is a versatile and thought-provoking author acclaimed for her gripping thrillers that delve into the complexities of crime, faith, and the human condition. Her writing spans a wide range of genres—including true crime, Christian devotionals, and socially conscious non-fiction—each work marked by a deep commitment to exposing injustice, championing reform, and unabashedly born-again Christian beliefs with a heart to pursue The Triune I Am God.

More than a storyteller, Lindsay uses her platform to provoke meaningful dialogue and drive systemic change. Whether addressing political, legislative, or religious issues, her narratives challenge the status quo and advocate for a more just, humane, and compassionate world. Her current projects include Christian Journals, and initiatives driven to enact protective domestic violence victim legislation, while living a purpose driven life as a storyteller of truths.

When weaving awareness-movement works, Lindsay strives to blend narrative power with a clear call to action in her true stories; blurred only to protect the victim from further victimization.

AN INVITATION

For those seeking healing, divine intimacy, and breakthroughs

Join the Movement!

Identity Heist and its companion book Divine Theft are just the beginning.

If you've been touched by these volumes and choose action over apathy as your next move, where would you turn next?

Do you have a story you'd like Lindsay to share? Will yours be her next book? Submit your story for Lindsay to breathe to life!

And if you'd like to receive updates or to move into community of action takers within the #movehopeforward awareness movement just visit:

https://lindsaymcguire.com

Or go to the QR code below.

What can you expect?

- Receive companion materials, and exclusive content and/ or courses

- Submit your story to be featured or co-written by Lindsay

- Be the first to know about new releases in The Identity Heist series and other Book series by Lindsay McGuire including the Carpenter's Call – Identity Restored Journal encounters

END OF THIS BOOK

'

COMPANION BOOKS &
DIVINE THEFT CONTAIN MORE

'

CHECK BACK FOR
MORE
TITLES
COMING
MOTHER'S DAY
2026